Java Hibernate Cookbook

Over 50 recipes to help you build dynamic and powerful real-time Java Hibernate applications

Yogesh Prajapati

Vishal Ranapariya

PUBLISHING

BIRMINGHAM - MUMBAI

Java Hibernate Cookbook

First published: September 2015

Production reference: 1110915

Published by Packt Publishing Ltd.
Livery Place
35 Livery Street
Birmingham B3 2PB, UK.

ISBN 978-1-78439-190-4

www.packtpub.com

Credits

Authors

Yogesh Prajapati

Vishal Ranapariya

Reviewers

Mathieu Nayrolles

Ravi Sharma

Umamaheswaran T.G

Commissioning Editor

Taron Pereira

Acquisition Editor

Kevin Colaco

Content Development Editor

Samantha Gonsalves

Technical Editor

Siddhesh Ghadi

Copy Editor

Shruti Iyer

Project Coordinator

Sanchita Mandal

Proofreader

Safis Editing

Indexer

Monica Ajmera Mehta

Graphics

Disha Haria

Production Coordinator

Nilesh R. Mohite

Cover Work

Nilesh R. Mohite

About the Authors

Yogesh Prajapati is a Java programmer. He has more than 4 years of experience in implementing enterprise web applications using J2EE technologies. Yogesh has experience in technologies and frameworks such as Spring, Hibernate, RESTful Web Services, and MongoDB.

He pursued a BCA from Ganpat University, Kherva, Gujarat, India. In 2011, Yogesh obtained a master's degree in computer application from Gujarat University, Gujarat, India.

Yogesh's expertise is not limited to a particular domain; he has worked with clients in the transportation, finance, and health care domains. Apart from this, he has had experience in GIS development and has also worked in the hospitality industry.

Yogesh has a blog, `http://kode12.com`, where he shares his knowledge of Java and other technologies. He is interested in contributing to open source technologies and is enthusiastic about building new products and services. You can follow Yogesh on his blog and on Linkedin at `http://in.linkedin.com/in/yogeshmprajapati`.

First, I would like to thank all those who helped me personally and professionally to complete this book.

I would also like to thank my wife, Varsha, for her valuable support as she understood me and helped me finish this book. I would like to extend a big thank you to my baby boy, Aarush. Apart from these two people, I would like to thank my parents, Manoj and Vina Prajapati, who continuously motivated me while writing. Also, I would like thank my sisters, Sonal and Shital, who always support me to fulfill my dreams.

Lastly, a special shout-out goes to god, who gives me the power to accomplish such tasks. Last but not least, I would like to extend a very special thanks to the Java and Hibernate technologies for making life easier.

Vishal Ranapariya is a Java developer. He has more than 4 years of experience in implementing enterprise web applications using J2EE technology. He has experience with technologies and frameworks such as Java, J2EE, Spring, Hibernate, RESTful web services, MongoDB, and Core Hadoop.

Vishal pursued a BCA from Gujarat University, Gujarat, India. In 2011, he obtained a master's degree in computer application from Gujarat University, Gujarat, India.

Vishal has blogs at `http://kode12.com`, where he shares his knowledge of Java-related open source technologies. He is interested in contributing to open source technologies. Vishal is enthusiastic about building new products and services. You can follow Vishal on his blog and on LinkedIn at `https://in.linkedin.com/in/vishalranapariya`.

Firstly, I would like to thank all those who helped me personally and professionally to complete this book. I would also like to thank my parents, who continuously motivated me while writing this book.

About the Reviewers

Mathieu Nayrolles was born in France and lived in a small village in Côte d'Azur for almost 15 years. He began his studies in computer science in France and continued with them in Montréal, Canada, where he now lives with his wife. Mathieu holds two master's degrees in eXia.Cesi (software engineering) and UQAM (computer science) respectively. He is now a PhD student at Concordia University (electrical and computer engineering), Montréal, Canada, under the supervision of Dr. Wahab Hamou-Lhadj.

Despite his academic journey, Mathieu has been consulting as a Magento performances specialist since the release of Magento 1.6 (August 2011) and has also worked for companies worldwide, such as Eurocopter and Saint-Gobain, where he learned how important good technical resources are.

You can discover some of Mathieu's work through his books, *Instant Magento Performance Optimization How-to*, *Magento Site Performance Optimization*, *Mastering Apache Solr*, and *Xamarin Studio for Android Programming: A C# Cookbook* or its latest editions, `https://bumper-app.com`, `https://mindup.io/` and `https://toolwatch.io/`.

You can follow Mathieu on Twitter at `@MathieuN1s`.

Ravi Sharma is a software professional with over 12 years of experience, working with various companies such as Oracle, Yahoo, and Tier-1 Banks and in the mobile advertising sector. He has mainly worked with Lower latency, which are highly transactional systems involving the processing of billions of requests per day and creating scalable systems.

Ravi received his BTech degree (honors) from YMCA Institute of Engineering, Faridabad, India. In the last few years, he has been a part of various political and social organisations (NGOs), where he has written on architecture and design and built systems for political organisations. Ravi has also built an e-governance system called eSwaraj (`http://www.eswaraj.com`).

Umamaheswaran T.G has more than 15 years of experience in information technology. He is a software architect at C1X (`www.c1exchange.com`), a fast growing start-up in the San Francisco Bay Area. Uma is an ex-Yahoo employee. Prior to that, he was a senior Java consultant for Wells Fargo USA, Citibank Japan, and various other clients.

Uma has also reviewed the following books for Packt Publishing:

- *Drools Developer's Cookbook*
- *Learning Informatica PowerCenter 9.x*

I would like to thank my wife, Chitra, and my two kids, Sivasweatha and Sivayogeith, for their support and cooperation.

www.PacktPub.com

Support files, eBooks, discount offers, and more

For support files and downloads related to your book, please visit www.PacktPub.com.

Did you know that Packt offers eBook versions of every book published, with PDF and ePub files available? You can upgrade to the eBook version at www.PacktPub.com and as a print book customer, you are entitled to a discount on the eBook copy. Get in touch with us at service@packtpub.com for more details.

At www.PacktPub.com, you can also read a collection of free technical articles, sign up for a range of free newsletters and receive exclusive discounts and offers on Packt books and eBooks.

https://www2.packtpub.com/books/subscription/packtlib

Do you need instant solutions to your IT questions? PacktLib is Packt's online digital book library. Here, you can search, access, and read Packt's entire library of books.

Why Subscribe?

- ▸ Fully searchable across every book published by Packt
- ▸ Copy and paste, print, and bookmark content
- ▸ On demand and accessible via a web browser

Free Access for Packt account holders

If you have an account with Packt at www.PacktPub.com, you can use this to access PacktLib today and view 9 entirely free books. Simply use your login credentials for immediate access.

Table of Contents

Preface

There are multiple databases available to store our valuable data. When we go for relational data structures, we can perform any operation on the data using queries on the interface provided by the database vendor or using a third party tool. The syntax for all databases is almost similar, but some databases follow their own syntax and semantics of writing a query. Nowadays, real-world applications require a quick development cycle, database-independent query execution, and a generic code that can be supported by multiple databases. It's a very hard and time-consuming task for a software developer to fulfill this set of requirements.

Hibernate is an ORM (Object Relational Mapping) tool that helps us by making our development process faster and making the software development independent of the database; so, we can easily change a database vendor without worrying about the changes required in code. Therefore, whether you are developing a standalone Java application or a server-side Java Enterprise application, you could use hibernate to make your code database-independent.

Java Hibernate Cookbook will help you to learn hibernate from the basics to an advanced level. In this book, we will try to create simple and short recipes to understand hibernate step by step.

What this book covers

Chapter 1, *Setting Up Hibernate*, provides the basics of hibernate and the persistent class. Next, you will learn to obtain the required libraries, XML and annotation-based configuration, and the mapping required for hibernate.

Chapter 2, *Understanding the Fundamentals*, takes you through the basic objects required to start working with hibernate, such as `SessionFactory`, `Session`, `Criteria`, `Projection`, and so on.

Chapter 3, *Basic Annotations*, covers the very basic annotations that are useful and necessary while writing with hibernate, such as declaring table (`@Table`), declaring column (`@Column`), declaring primary key (`@Id`), and so on.

Chapter 4, Working with Collections, explains how collections work with hibernate and how to persist Java collections such as `List`, `Map`, `Set`, and so on using hibernate.

Chapter 5, Working With Associations, helps you to understand relationships and associations such as one-to-one, one-to-many (many-to-one), and many-to-many. In this chapter, you will discover the simplest way to implement a relationship using hibernate.

Chapter 6, Querying, applies the basics of hibernate to query a database. This chapter helps you to understand the fundamentals of hibernate such as alias, subquery, NamedQuery, formula, and HQL.

Chapter 7, Advanced Concepts, helps you to learn the advanced concepts in hibernate such as caching, inheritance strategy, versioning, and maintaining the history of the objects.

Chapter 8, Integration with Other Frameworks, explains integration with other MVC frameworks such as Struts and Spring. It shows how to achieve a persistent life cycle in the frameworks.

What you need for this book

Knowledge of the Java programming language is a must. Also, you are expected to have an understanding of the relational database, SQL query, and JDBC API. The knowledge of IDEs such as Eclipse or NetBeans is preferred.

You will need the following software/tools:

- JDK 6
- Eclipse IDE
- Maven
- Hibernate 3.6.7 JAR
- MySQL Database Server
- JDBC Driver for MySQL
- Hibernate Envers

Who this book is for

This is book for the Java developers who now want to learn hibernate. A good knowledge and understanding of Java is preferred to allow an efficient programming of the core elements and applications. It would also be helpful if the readers are familiar with the basics of SQL.

Sections

In this book, you will find several headings that appear frequently (Getting ready, How to do it, How it works, There's more, and See also).

To give clear instructions on how to complete a recipe, we use these sections as follows:

Getting ready

This section tells you what to expect in the recipe and describes how to set up any software or any other preliminary settings required for the recipe.

How to do it...

This section contains the steps required to follow the recipe.

How it works...

This section usually consists of a detailed explanation of what happened in the previous section.

There's more...

This section consists of any additional information about the recipe in order to make the reader more knowledgeable about the recipe.

See also

This section provides helpful links to other useful information for the recipe.

Conventions

In this book, you will find a number of text styles that distinguish between different kinds of information. Here are some examples of these styles and an explanation of their meaning.

Code words in text, database table names, folder names, filenames, file extensions, pathnames, dummy URLs, user input, and Twitter handles are shown as follows: "`dialect` helps hibernate to generate database specific SQL statements."

A block of code is set as follows:

```
<hibernate-mapping>
  <class="Employee" table="employee">
    <id name="id" type="long" column="id">
      <generator class="increment" />
    </id>
    <property column="firstName" name="firstName" />
    <property column="salary" name="salary" />
  </class>
</hibernate-mapping>
```

When we wish to draw your attention to a particular part of a code block, the relevant lines or items are set in bold:

```
@AuditTable(value="emp_history")
public class Employee {
  // other fields and setters/getters
}
```

> 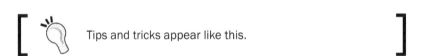 Warnings or important notes appear in a box like this.

> Tips and tricks appear like this.

Reader feedback

Feedback from our readers is always welcome. Let us know what you think about this book—what you liked or disliked. Reader feedback is important for us as it helps us develop titles that you will really get the most out of.

To send us general feedback, simply e-mail `feedback@packtpub.com`, and mention the book's title in the subject of your message.

If there is a topic that you have expertise in and you are interested in either writing or contributing to a book, see our author guide at `www.packtpub.com/authors`.

Customer support

Now that you are the proud owner of a Packt book, we have a number of things to help you to get the most from your purchase.

Downloading the example code

You can download the example code files from your account at `http://www.packtpub.com` for all the Packt Publishing books you have purchased. If you purchased this book elsewhere, you can visit `http://www.packtpub.com/support` and register to have the files e-mailed directly to you.

Errata

Although we have taken every care to ensure the accuracy of our content, mistakes do happen. If you find a mistake in one of our books—maybe a mistake in the text or the code—we would be grateful if you could report this to us. By doing so, you can save other readers from frustration and help us improve subsequent versions of this book. If you find any errata, please report them by visiting `http://www.packtpub.com/submit-errata`, selecting your book, clicking on the **Errata Submission Form** link, and entering the details of your errata. Once your errata are verified, your submission will be accepted and the errata will be uploaded to our website or added to any list of existing errata under the Errata section of that title.

To view the previously submitted errata, go to `https://www.packtpub.com/books/content/support` and enter the name of the book in the search field. The required information will appear under the **Errata** section.

Piracy

Piracy of copyrighted material on the Internet is an ongoing problem across all media. At Packt, we take the protection of our copyright and licenses very seriously. If you come across any illegal copies of our works in any form on the Internet, please provide us with the location address or website name immediately so that we can pursue a remedy.

Please contact us at `copyright@packtpub.com` with a link to the suspected pirated material.

We appreciate your help in protecting our authors and our ability to bring you valuable content.

Questions

If you have a problem with any aspect of this book, you can contact us at `questions@packtpub.com`, and we will do our best to address the problem.

1
Setting Up Hibernate

In this chapter, we will cover the following recipes:

- ▶ Getting the required libraries for hibernate
- ▶ Creating a hibernate persistent class
- ▶ Providing an XML-based hibernate mapping
- ▶ Providing an annotation-based hibernate mapping
- ▶ Providing a hibernate configuration using an XML file
- ▶ Providing a hibernate configuration using a properties file
- ▶ Configuring hibernate programmatically

Introduction

In this chapter, we will take a look at how the hibernate and **ORM (Object-relational Mapping)** frameworks work, how to configure hibernate in different ways, and the libraries that are required for the hibernate application. An essential part of the application is the hibernate configuration. Through the configuration, we can provide database information to the hibernate engine, such as the database host, port, username, password, the database name, the drive class, and so on.

In the older era of Java development, developers used some methodologies to persist data. To persist data means to save or store data in some storage medium by maintaining it in a certain state. Once the data is successfully persisted, it can be used at any given time. A database is the more preferable storage medium for a transactional operation. Usually, we use **JDBC (Java Database Connectivity)** to perform such operation with the database.

If we use the JDBC operation, we need to work a bit harder and take care of the following processes:

- Opening a database connection
- Maintaining an open connection
- Building a query
- Executing a query
- Getting a response to the query
- Mapping the query response with the custom classes
- Closing the database connection

To avoid this hectic process, we can use the ORM tools available in the market. ORM stands for Object Relation Mapping. It works as a bridge between the application and database by simplifying the communication between them.

The benefits of the ORM framework are as follows:

- It reduces the development time/cost.
- It speeds up the development.
- It provides us with portability. Hibernate supports multiple databases, so there is no need to write a database-specific code.

This is a useful feature of hibernate. Generally, all databases have their own syntax made up of **Data Definition Language** (**DDL**) or **Data Manipulation Language** (**DML**) statements. If we used JDBC, we would need to write a database-specific code as our database is changed. However, hibernate gets rid of the developer's headache by handling this issue.

The syntax of a query may be different for different database parameters; still, hibernate works in the same way for all types of databases. Hibernate's term `dialect` helps achieve this type of functionality. The implementation of the `dialect` class is provided by the database provider to inform hibernate about the syntax of this particular database.

Some useful features of hibernate are as follows:

- Code reusability
- Transaction management
- Efficient collection/custom classes mapping
- The caching mechanism supported by hibernate

Getting the required libraries for hibernate

To work with hibernate, we need a **JAR** (**Java Archive**) file provided by hibernate. Here, we will see how to download the hibernate core distribution. There are multiple ways to get the required libraries; here, we will consider two of them:

- Manually downloading
- Using Maven

Manually downloading

The first and most basic JAR file needed is a JDBC driver. The JDBC driver is a bridge or an API between Java and the database. The JDBC driver provides us with the generic classes that will help us communicate with the database. Generally, the driver is either provided by the database provider or developed by communities; however, you have to get it yourself. This also depends on the type of the database you are using. As we will use the MySQL database for this book, we will use the `Mysql-Connector.jar` file.

How to do it...

Let's come back to the library section. Apart from JDBC, you will need the JAR files for hibernate. Perform the following steps:

1. Download the hibernate core distribution from `http://hibernate.org/orm/`.

2. Now, place all the files in your classpath if you plan to run a standalone program and put them in the `lib` folder if it's a J2EE project.

 When you manually download the libraries, it's the programmer's responsibility to get all the required and dependent JAR files from the official site of hibernate; failing this, they will face errors.

Using Maven

If you use the Maven project, it would get rid of your headache of finding all the JAR files for hibernate and the dependent libraries. You can use the following Maven configuration for hibernate.

How to do it...

1. Enter the following code into the `pom.xml` source file to show the dependency mapping of hibernate and MySQL in `pom.xml`:

```
...
<dependencies>
  <!-- MySQL connector -->
  <dependency>
    <groupId>MySQL</groupId>
    <artifactId>MySQL-connector-Java</artifactId>
    <version>MySQL-connector-version</version>
  </dependency>

  <!-- Hibernate framework -->
  <dependency>
    <groupId>hibernate</groupId>
    <artifactId>hibernate-core</artifactId>
    <version>hibernate-version</version>
  </dependency>
<dependencies>
```

Using this method, Maven will download all the required JAR files related to hibernate and the dependent libraries required for hibernate.

 Replace MySQL-connector-version with your required MySQL connector version in the `<version>MySQL-connector-version</version>` line, and replace hibernate-version with your required hibernate version in the `<version>hibernate-version</version>` line.

Creating a hibernate persistent class

As discussed in the *Preface*, the developer will be dealing with objects at every step of development. Also, when we use hibernate, we don't need to work on a core SQL query. Here, we will create a **POJO (Plain Old Java Object)** in Java, which represents a table in the database.

Getting ready

By POJO, we mean that we will create a Java class that satisfies the following requirements:

▶   It needs to have a default constructor that is persistent.

▶   It should contain the `id` attribute. ID is used to identify the object and is mapped with the primary column of a table.

▶   All attributes should have `Getter` and `Setter` methods, such as `getXXX` and `setXXX` where xxx is a field name.

How to do it...

We will now create a persistent class and name it `Employee`. The following table shows a representation of the `Employee` class:

Employee
id
firstName
salary

1. Create the `Employee.java` class and place the following code in the class:

```java
public class Employee{
   private long id;
   private String firstName;
   private double salary;
   // other fields

   // default constructor
   public Employee() {
   }

   public long getId() {
        return id;
   }

   public void setId(long id) {
      this.id = id;
   }

   public String getFirstName() {
      return firstName;
   }

   public void setFirstName(String firstName) {
      this.firstName = firstName;
   }

   public double getSalary() {
      return salary;
   }

   public void setSalary(double salary) {
      this.salary = salary;
```

```
        }

        //
        // Getter and setter for other fields...
        //

    }
```

Now the preceding class satisfies all the requirements listed before to be a persistent class.

The preceding class now contains the following:

- The default `Employee()` constructor
- The `id` attribute, which is the primary column of the table and can be used to uniquely identify an entry
- The individual getters and setters in all the attributes (`id`, `firstName`, and `salary`)

There's more...

Now, let's see how to design a POJO for tables having references between the `Department` and `Employee` tables:

Department	Employee
id	id
deptName	firstName
	salary
	department

The following code is the definition for the `Department` class in `Department.java`:

```
public class Department{
    private long id;
    private String deptName;

    //default constructor
    public void Department(){
    }

    //getters and setters
    public long getId() {
        return id;
    }

    public void setId(long id) {
```

```
      this.id = id;
   }

   public String getDeptName() {
      return deptName;
   }

   public void setDeptName(String deptName) {
      this.deptName = deptName;
   }

}
```

The following code is the definition for the `Employee` class in `Employee.java`:

```
public class Employee{
   private long id;
   private String firstName;
   private double salary;
   private Department department; // reference to Department.

   //default constructor
   public void Employee(){
   }

   //getters and setters
   public long getId() {
      return id;
   }

   public void setId(long id) {
      this.id = id;
   }

   public String getFirstName() {
      return firstName;
   }

   public void setFirstName(String firstName) {
      this.firstName = firstName;
   }

   public double getSalary() {
      return salary;
   }
```

```
public void setSalary(double salary) {
  this.salary = salary;
}

public Department getDepartment(){
  return department;
}

public setDepartment(Department department){
  this.department = department;
}

}
```

Downloading the example code

You can download the example code files for all Packt books you have purchased from your account at http://www.packtpub.com. If you purchased this book elsewhere, you can visit http://www.packtpub.com/support and register to have the files e-mailed directly to you.

Providing an XML-based hibernate mapping

In the preceding recipe, you learned how to create a POJO. Now we will consider how to create the configuration for hibernate. There are multiple ways of mapping, and this is one of them.

Generally, the configuration provides the following information:

- The mapping between the POJO and the database table
- The mapping between the POJO property and the database table column
- The definition of the primary key column
- The definitions of the foreign key column and relationships such as one-to-one, one-to-many, many-to-one, many-to-many with another table, and so on
- Constraints such as not-null, formula, lazy, cascade, and so on
- The definitions of the length, the data type of the column, the formula, and so on

How to do it...

To provide hibernate mapping based on XML, perform the following steps:

1. Ensure that the basic structure of the configuration file is as follows:

```
<!DOCTYPE hibernate-mapping PUBLIC
"-//Hibernate/Hibernate Mapping DTD X.X//EN"
"http://hibernate.sourceforge.net/hibernate-mapping-
X.X.dtd">
<hibernate-mapping>
...
</hibernate-mapping>
```

 We have not provided the DTD code for the future demo in this book, but it should be present while developing.

2. Create a XML file and name it `Employee.hbm.xml`. Then, add the configuration, as shown in the following code:

```
<hibernate-mapping>
  <class="Employee" table="employee">
    <id name="id" type="long" column="id">
      <generator class="increment" />
    </id>
    <property column="firstName" name="firstName" />
    <property column="salary" name="salary" />
    <!-- other properties mapping-->
  </class>
</hibernate-mapping>
```

 Here, we named the mapping file `Employee.hbm.xml`. However, while developing, there is no strict rule regarding the naming convention. Here, we will create a new hbm file for each POJO; for example, we created an `Employee.hbm.xml` file for the `Employee.java` class. Another common practice we will use here is to create one hbm file for the module, map all the classes of this module in the same mapping file, and name this file `modulename.hbm.xml`.

How it works...

Here, `<hibernate-mapping>` is a root element that contains all the `<class>` elements. The `<class>` tag contains the following attributes:

▶ name: This specifies the **FQN** (**Fully Qualified Name**) of the Java class.

- ▶ `table`: This denotes the database table used for the class defined in the `name` attribute.

- ▶ The `<generator>` tag in the `<id>` tag is used to generate the value of the primary key. There are many types of built-in generators provided by hibernate, such as `identity`, `sequence`, `hilo`, and so on.

The `<id>` tag defines the primary key column for the database table. It contains the following attributes:

- ▶ `name`: This specifies the Java class attribute name

- ▶ `column`: This denotes the database table's column name

- ▶ `type`: This specifies the data type of the column that will help hibernate during the creation and retrieval of the automatic table

- ▶ `size`: This denotes the size attribute that defines the length of the table's column

> The `type` attribute in the `<id>` and `<property>` tags helps hibernate to create a table structure automatically for us using the hbm mapping.

Usually, we create a mapping file called **hbm** (**hibernate mapping**). It is a normal XML schema file that contains custom hibernate XML tags. This helps the hibernate engine to map the class to the table and the `class` field to the `table` column, along with the given attributes.

All the mapping definitions for hibernate are bundled under the `<hibernate-mapping>` ... `</hibernate-mapping>` tag. In `<hibernate-mapping>` ... `</hibernate-mapping>`, we can add any number of class-to-table mapping definitions.

> It is good practice to provide the type in mapping because if this attribute is not provided, hibernate needs to use reflection to get the data type of the field; reflection requires a little more processing than a normal execution does.

There's more...

Now, let's create the XML mapping for the POJO having a reference with another POJO. Here, we will create two different mapping files. To achieve this using an XML-based mapping, we have to create different class mappings for each POJO that has a dependency.

The following is a code that represents the mapping for the `Department` class. The mapping is in the `Department.hbm.xml` file:

```
...
<hibernate-mapping>
```

```
    <class name="Department" table="department">
      <id name="id" type="long" column="id">
        <generator class="auto" />
      </id>

      <property column="deptName" name="deptName" />
      <!-- other properties mapping -->
    </class>
  </hibernate-mapping>
  ...
```

Next, we will create a mapping for the `Employee` class. Its definition is present in the `Employee.hbm.xml` file:

```
  ...
  <hibernate-mapping>
    <class="Employee" table="employee">
      <id name="id" type="long" column="id">
        <generator class="auto" />
      </id>

      <property column="firstName" name="firstName" />
      <property column="salary" name="salary" />
      <many-to-one name="department" class="Department" >
        <column name="department"/>
      </many-to-one>
      <!-- other properties mapping-->
    </class>
  </hibernate-mapping>
  ...
```

In the preceding example, we mapped the `Department` entity with the `Employee` entity. This will refer to the `department` column in the employee table. This means that it will create a foreign key that is referenced to the department table.

Here, we will use the `<many-to-one>` relationship, which means that either many employees are connected with one department, or one department is used by many employees.

The properties are as follows:

▶ not-null="`true`": This property prevents the user from inserting the NULL value in the column

▶ lazy="`true`": This feature helps us while retrieving data using hibernate

The two possible options for `lazy` are `true` and `false`. In our example, `Employee` is a parent class, whereas `Department` is a child of the `Employee` class. Now, while fetching, if we set `lazy` as `true`, it means that it will only fetch employee records. No child records will be fetched with `Employee`, and hibernate will use a separate query if we try to access a child record, which is `employee.getDepartment()`. If we set `lazy` as `false`, hibernate will fetch the child records with the parent, which means that the department information will also be fetched, along with that of the employee. Hibernate will use a join query to fetch the child records.

Providing an annotation-based hibernate mapping

When we choose the annotation-based way to provide a configuration, we don't need to create any hibernate mapping (usually `*.hbm. xml`) file. Hibernate provides the annotations that we can directly write to the POJO, and we can provide all the mappings via the classes, which we can do using the previous XML file.

How to do it...

Now, let's create the class that contains the annotation-based mapping. As we used the `Employee` class to provide XML-based mapping here, we will use the same class with annotations:

1. Represent the annotation-based mapping for the `Employee` class in `Employee.java`, as shown in the following code:

```java
import javax.persistence.Column;
import javax.persistence.Entity;
import javax.persistence.GeneratedValue;
import javax.persistence.Id;
import javax.persistence.Table;

@Entity
@Table(name="employee")
public class Employee{

    @Id
    @Column(name="id")
    @GeneratedValue(strategy = GenerationType.AUTO)
    private long id;

    @Column(name="firstname")
    private String firstName;
```

```
@Column(name = "salary")
private double salary;

// default constructor
public Employee() {
}

public long getId() {
  return id;
}

public void setId(long id) {
  this.id = id;
}

public String getFirstName() {
    return firstName;
}

public void setFirstName(String firstName) {
  this.firstName = firstName;
}

public double getSalary() {
  return salary;
}

public void setSalary(double salary) {
  this.salary = salary;
}

}
```

How it works...

Now, compare the annotations with the XML mapping to gain a better understanding of the difference between the two methods.

Declaring a class — Table for the database

In the annotations, we will write the following code:

```
@Entity
@Table(name="employee")
public class Employee{...}
```

Now, check the XML mapping for the same here:

```
<class name="Employee" table="employee">
```

The keywords used in the preceding class are described below:

▸ `@Entity`: This annotation declares the class as an entity bean.

▸ `@Table`: We can set this annotation at the class level only. You can provide the `name` attribute, which is considered as a database table name. You can also just write `@Table` without any attribute; in this case, the class name is considered as a table name by hibernate.

Declaring an ID — The primary key for the table

In the annotations, we will write the following code:

```
@Id
@Column(name="id")
@GeneratedValue(strategy = GenerationType.AUTO)
private long id;
```

Now, check the XML mapping for the same in the following code:

```
<id name="id" type="long" column="id">
  <generator class="auto" />
</id>
```

The annotations used in the preceding code are described below:

▸ `@Id`: This annotation declares the property to be an identifier property, and this is used as a primary key for the table.

▸ `@Column`: This annotation is used to define the `column` for the table. Here, we used `name="id"`, meaning that hibernate considers the column name to be `"id"`. You can also write `@Column` without any attributes; in this case, the property name is considered to be a column name for the table.

▸ `@GeneratedValue`: Using this annotation, we can provide information to hibernate on how to generate a value for the primary key column. Here, we will use `strategy = GenerationType.AUTO`, which means that hibernate uses the autoincrement value for the `id` column. If not provided, hibernate uses the most appropriate generation strategy.

Referencing an object

In the annotations, we will write the following code:

```
@JoinColumn(name="department")
@ManyToOne
private Department department;
```

Now check the XML mapping for the same in the following code:

```
<many-to-one name="department" class="Department">
  <column name="department"/>
</many-to-one>
```

The annotations used in the preceding code are described below:

▸ @JoinColumn: This annotation notifies hibernate that this is a reference column.

▸ @ManyToOne: This annotation defines the relation between the referenced tables. Here, we have used many-to-one, meaning that one department can be mapped with multiple employees.

There's more...

In the previous section you learned how to reference a class using hibernate. In this section, we will take a look at how to provide the reference of one class in another class in detail.

Do not get confused when writing Employee.java again to show the reference object annotation.

The following code represents the annotation-based mapping for the Employee class that has the reference field in Employee.java:

```
import javax.persistence.Column;
import javax.persistence.Entity;
import javax.persistence.GeneratedValue;
import javax.persistence.Id;
import javax.persistence.ManyToOne;
import javax.persistence.Table;

@Entity
@Table(name="employee")
public class Employee{

    @Id
    @Column(name="id")
    @GeneratedValue(strategy = GenerationType.AUTO)
    private long id;

    @Column(name="firstname")
    private String firstName;

    @Column(name = "salary")
    private double salary;
```

```
    @JoinColumn(name="department")
    @ManyToOne
    private Department department;

    // default constructor
    public Employee() {
    }

    // getters & setters
    public long getId() {
    return id;
    }

    public void setId(long id) {
    this.id = id;
    }

    public String getFirstName() {
    return firstName;
    }

    public void setFirstName(String firstName) {
    this.firstName = firstName;
    }

    public double getSalary() {
    return salary;
    }

    public void setSalary(double salary) {
    this.salary = salary;
    }

    public Department getDepartment(){
    return department;
    }

  public setDepartment(Department department){
    this.department = department;
  }
}
```

The following code represents the annotation-based mapping for the `Department` class in `Department.java`:

```java
import javax.persistence.Column;
import javax.persistence.Entity;
import javax.persistence.GeneratedValue;
import javax.persistence.Id;
import javax.persistence.Table;

@Entity
@Table //If name is not supplied hibernate will use class name as
table name
public class Department{
  @Id
  @Column //If name is not supplied hibernate will use field name
as column name
  @GeneratedValue(strategy = GenerationType.AUTO)
  private long id;

  @Column
  private String deptName;

  public long getId() {
    return id;
  }

  public void setId(long id) {
    this.id = id;
  }

  public String getDeptName() {
    return deptName;
  }

  public void setDeptName(String deptName) {
    this.deptName = deptName;
  }

}
```

Providing a hibernate configuration using an XML file

In the preceding discussion, you learned how to create a class and provide a mapping to hibernate. These mappings show the relationship between the Java class and the database table.

Still, hibernate requires some information about the database, host, and port, on which the application is running. It also requires information about the username and password to access the database. Hibernate uses this set of configurations to connect to the database.

This is a traditional way to provide the hibernate configuration; however here, we need to create an XML file, generally called `hibernate.cfg.xml`, in the classpath. There is no strict rule to name it `hibernate.cfg.xml`; we can give it a custom name instead of `hibernate.cfg.xml`, in which case, we need to instruct hibernate to load the configuration from the particular file. Otherwise, hibernate looks for the file named `hibernate.cfg.xml` in the classpath.

How to do it...

Now, we will create the XML file that shows the configuration for MySQL:

1. Enter the following code in `hibernate.cfg.xml` to show the configuration for the applications:

```
...
<hibernate-configuration>
  <session-factory>

    <property name="hibernate.dialect">
      org.hibernate.dialect.MySQLDialect
    </property>
    <property name="hibernate.connection.driver_class">
      com.mysql.jdbc.Driver
    </property>
    <property name="hibernate.connection.url">
      jdbc:mysql://localhost:3306/kode12
    </property>
    <property name="hibernate.connection.username">
      root
    </property>
    <property name="hibernate.connection.password">
      root
    </property>
    <property name="show_sql">true</property>
```

```
    <property name="hbm2ddl.auto">update</property>

    <!-- List of XML mapping files -->
    <mapping resource="Employee.hbm.xml"/>
    <mapping resource="Department.hbm.xml"/>

    </session-factory>
</hibernate-configuration>
```

How it works...

Here, we will take a look at only the basic configuration parameters. Let's understand the meaning of each property:

- `<property name="hibernate.dialect">org.hibernate.dialect. MySQLDialect</property>`: This property helps hibernate to generate database-specific SQL statements. This is an optional property. According to hibernate documentation, hibernate will be able to choose the correct implementation of `dialect` automatically using the JDBC metadata returned by the JDBC driver.

- `<property name="hibernate.connection.driver_class">com.mysql. jdbc.Driver</property>`: Using this property, we can provide the **Fully Qualified Name** (**FQN**) of the java `driver` name for a particular database. The `driver` class is implemented using Java and resides in the JAR file and contains the driver that should be placed in our classpath.

- `<property name="hibernate.connection.url">jdbc:mysql:// localhost:3306/kode12</property>`: Using this property, we can provide the physical location of the database; however, the connection URL may vary from database to database. Here, we will use the MySQL database, so the URL shows `jdbc:MySQL://<host/computer-name/ip>:<port>/<database name to connect>`.

- `<property name="hibernate.connection.username">root</property>`: Using this property, we can provide the username to access a particular database.

- `<property name="hibernate.connection.password">root</property>`: Using this property, we can provide the password to access a particular database.

- `<property name="show_sql">true</property>`: The possible value for this property is either `true` or `false`. This is an optional property. Hibernate logs all the generated queries that reach the database to the console if the value of `show_sql` is set to `true`. This is useful during basic troubleshooting. Hibernate will use the prepared statement so that it does not display the parameter in the output window. If you want to see this parameter as well, you will have to enable the detailed log. Log4j is preferred for the detailed log.

▶ `<property name="hbm2ddl.auto">create</property>`: The possible values are `validate`, `update`, `create` or `create-drop`. This is also an optional property. Here, we will set value=`create` so that it will remove all the schemas and create a new one using the hibernate mapping on each build of `sessionfactory`. For value=`update`, hibernate will update the new changes in the database.

 Do not use the `hbm2ddl.auto` property in the production environment because it may remove all of the data and schema. So, it's best practice to avoid it in the production environment.

▶ `<mapping resource="Employee.hbm.xml"/>`: All of the mapping file is declared in the `mapping` tag, and the mapping file is always named `xx.hbm.xml`. We can use multiple mapping tags for multiple mapping files.

Here is an example:

```
<mapping resource="Employee.hbm.xml"/>
<mapping resource="Department.hbm.xml"/>
```

There's more...

Here are some useful properties used in hibernate:

▶ `hibernate.format_sql`:

  ❑ The possible values are `true` and `false`

  ❑ It shows the hibernate-generated queries in the pretty format if set as `true`

▶ `hibernate.connection.pool_size`:

  ❑ The possible value is always greater than 1 (`value >= 1`)

  ❑ It limits the maximum number of pooled connections

▶ `hibernate.connection.autocommit`:

  ❑ The possible values are `true` and `false`

  ❑ It sets the `autocommit` mode for JDBC

Providing a hibernate configuration using the properties file

This is another way to configure hibernate; here, we will create a file with the `.properties` extension. Usually called `hibernate.properties`, this file is a replacement for `hibernate.cfg.xml`. You can use any approach (either `cfg.xml` or the properties file). However, the properties file is better for startup, and it is the easiest approach to get started quickly.

This is a simpler representation of an XML file. Hibernate searches for the XML file or the properties file at startup to find the configuration in your classpath. We can use any one of these options. You can use both of them at the same time, but this is uncommon because hibernate gives priority to the XML file over properties; the properties file is simply ignored in such cases.

> The properties file looks similar to a normal text file, but the content should be in a key/value pair, which is `Key=Value`.
>
> Here is an example: `hibernate.connection.driver_class=com.mysql.jdbc.Driver`.

How to do it...

Now, we will create a file called `hibernate.properties` in our classpath and write the following properties in the file. The following code represents `hibernate.cfg.xml` in the `hibernate.properties` file:

```
...
hibernate.dialect=org.hibernate.dialect.MySQLDialect
hibernate.connection.driver_class=com.mysql.jdbc.Driver
hibernate.connection.url=jdbc:mysql://localhost:3306/kode12
hibernate.connection.username=root
hibernate.connection.password=root
show_sql=true
hbm2ddl.auto=update
...
```

How it works...

When we create an instance of the `Configuration` class, it will look for `hibernate.cfg.xml` or `hibernate.properties` in our classpath. If we use a `.properties` file, it'll get all of the property defined in the file, rather than create a `Configuration` object.

> The difference between an XML and properties file is that, in an XML file, you can directly map classes using the `<Mapping>` tag, but there is no way to configure it in a properties file. So, you can use this methodology when you use a programmatic configuration.

Configuring hibernate programmatically

In the preceding section, we understood XML and the properties-based configuration. Hibernate also supports the programmatic configuration. To configure hibernate using this method, we have to work on a Java code and create an instance of the `org.hibernate.cfg.Configuration` class. There are multiple ways to configure hibernate.

How to do it...

First, write the following code:

```
Configuration configuration = new Configuration();
```

This will create an instance of the `Configuration` class using `hibernate.cfg.xml` or `hibernate.properties`, whichever is found in the classpath.

Provide the following mapping files to the configuration:

```
configuration = configuration.addResource("Employee.hbm.xml");
configuration = configuration.addResource("Department.hbm.xml");
```

You can use an alternate way, as shown in the following code:

```
Configuration configuration = new
Configuration().addResource("Employee.hbm.xml").addResource("Depar
tment.hbm.xml");
```

We can also provide a direct mapping using the class, as shown in the following code:

```
configuration = configuration.addClass("Department.class");
```

This will also look for `Department.hbm.xml`.

We can also set a custom property. To set up the custom property, use the following method:

```
configuration.setProperty(propertyName, value);
```

For example, consider the following code:

```
configuration.setProperty("show_sql", true);
```

To set up multiple properties using the properties object, execute the following code:

```
configuration.setProperties(java.util.Properties properties);
```

Here is an example:

```
Properties properties = new Properties();
properties.put("hibernate.dialect",
"org.hibernate.dialect.MySQLDialect");
properties.put("hibernate.connection.driver_class",
"com.mysql.jdbc.Driver");
properties.put("hibernate.connection.url",
"jdbc:mysql://localhost:3306/kode12");
properties.put("hibernate.connection.username", "root");
properties.put("hibernate.connection.password", "root");
properties.put("show_sql", "true");
properties.put("hbm2ddl.auto", "update");
configuration.setProperties(properties);
```

To read the mapping from the URL, you can use the following code:

```
configuration = configuration.addURL(java.net.URL url);
```

To read the mapping from the XML file, you can use the following code:

```
configuration = configuration.addXML(String xml);
```

How it works...

When we select the programmatic configuration option, the `Configuration` class is very important. Using the instance of the `Configuration` class, we will build a `SessionFactory` object, as shown in the following code:

```
SessionFactory sessionFactory = new
Configuration().buildSessionFactory();
```

When the preceding code is executed, it creates a `SessionFactory` object using a `.properties` or `.cfg` file or whichever source is provided to create the configuration.

2
Understanding the Fundamentals

In this chapter, we will cover the following recipes:

- Building a `SessionFactory`
- Creating a generic `SessionFactory` provider class
- Opening a new session
- Opening a stateless session
- Saving an object to the database
- Fetching an object from the database
- Removing an object from the database
- Updating an object
- Creating a criteria
- Restricting the results using a criteria
- Pagination using a criteria
- Sorting the results
- Transforming a result
- Using basic projection

Introduction

Before we proceed, it's necessary to learn about the fundamentals of hibernate: the classes and interfaces required.

In this chapter, we will cover the fundamentals of hibernate, such as `SessionFactory`, `Session`, and `Criteria`. We will discuss the importance of `SessionFactory` in the hibernate application. Criteria is used to do the actual transaction or the **CRUD** (**Create, Read, Update, Delete**) operation. Apart from this, we will cover some basic and useful functionalities, such as the sorting of results, limiting the number of rows, transforming a result, and the basics of projections.

Building a SessionFactory

First, we will discuss `SessionFactory` and how to create it in detail. As the name suggests, a `SessionFactory` is a factory of sessions.

A `SessionFactory` has the following features:

- It's an interface implemented using the singleton pattern.
- It's created using the configuration provided by the configuration file.
- It's thread-safe, so it's created once during the application's lifetime, and multiple users or threads can access it at the same time without any concurrency issue.
- As a `SessionFactory` object is immutable, changes made to the configuration will not affect the existing factory object.
- It's a factory class, and its main duty is to create, manage, and retrieve a session on request. A `Session` is used to get a physical connectivity with the database.

How to do it...

If you are using a version of hibernate that is earlier than 4, use the following code to create a `SessionFactory`:

```
/* Line 1 */ Configuration cfg = new Configuration();
/* Line 2 */ cfg = cfg.configure();
/* Line 3 */ SessionFactory sessionFactory =
cfg.buildSessionFactory();
```

As the `buildSessionFactory()` method of the `Configuration` class is deprecated in the version 4 of hibernate, you can use the following code to create a `SessionFactory`:

```
/* Line 1 */ Configuration configuration = new Configuration();
/* Line 2 */ configuration = configuration.configure();
```

```
/* Line 3 */ StandardServiceRegistryBuilder builder = new
StandardServiceRegistryBuilder();
/* Line 4 */ builder =
builder.applySettings(configuration.getProperties());
/* Line 5 */SessionFactory sessionFactory =
configuration.buildSessionFactory(builder.build());
```

How it works...

First of all, let's understand the code from the beginning.

When `Line 1` with the `Configuration cfg = new Configuration();` code is executed, it creates a blank `configuration`.

When `Line 2` with `cfg = cfg.configure();` is executed, the `configure()` method will look for the `hibernate.cfg.xml` or `hibernate.properties` file and then fetch all the properties defined in the configuration and mapping files and filled out in the `configuration` object.

When `Line 3` with `SessionFactory sessionFactory = cfg.buildSessionFactory();` is executed, the preceding code builds `SessionFactory` using the `Configuration` object. It actually creates the `SessionFactory` object using the configuration loaded in `Line 2`.

For the second part of the code, do the same thing. However, as the API is different, you need to create an instance of `StandardServiceRegistryBuilder` in `Line 3`, which works as a builder of the `ServiceRegistry` interface.

In `Line 4`, apply all the settings that are loaded into the configuration object. In the last line, `Line 5`, create an object of `SessionFactory`, the configuration being set by the builder itself.

There's more...

If we want to connect two different databases in an application, we need to create two different `SessionFactory` objects in it. Let's see how to do this.

For example, if we have two different databases, MySQL and PostgreSQL, we will create two different CFG files called `mysql.cfg.xml` and `postgresql.cfg.xml`. Then, we will just create a `SessionFactory`, as shown in the following code:

```
Configuration configurationMySQL = new
Configuration().configure("mysql.cfg.xml");
SessionFactory sessionFactoryMySQL = configurationMySQL
.buildSessionFactory();
```

```
Configuration configurationPostgresql = new
Configuration().configure("postgresql.cfg.xml");
SessionFactory sessionFactoryPostgresql = configurationPostgresql
.buildSessionFactory();
```

Now, we have two different `SessionFactory` objects that we can use as per our requirement.

Creating a generic SessionFactory provider class

Now, we will create a helper class, which will help us to set and get `SessionFactory` on demand.

We require `SessionFactory` at every point while working with hibernate. So, we will create a `HibernateUtil.java` class.

 This is just a naming convention and not a hibernate standard but is used globally by developers and communities for the ease of use.

How to do it...

Here, we will create a Java file with the name `HibernateUtil.java`:

1. Enter the following code in the `HibernateUtil.java` file:

```
import org.hibernate.SessionFactory;
import org.hibernate.cfg.Configuration;

public class HibernateUtil {
  private static final SessionFactory sessionFactory;

  static {
    try {
      // Create the SessionFactory from hibernate.cfg.xml
      sessionFactory = new
Configuration().configure().buildSessionFactory();

      // Use code below for Hibernate version 4
      // Configuration configuration = new Configuration();
      // configuration = configuration.configure();
      // StandardServiceRegistryBuilder builder = new
StandardServiceRegistryBuilder();
      // builder =
builder.applySettings(configuration.getProperties());
```

```
    // SessionFactory sessionFactory = configuration.
buildSessionFactory(builder.build());
    } catch (Throwable ex) {
        // Log the exception.
        System.err.println("SessionFactory creation failed."
+ ex);
        throw new ExceptionInInitializerError(ex);
    }
  }

  public static SessionFactory getSessionFactory() {
    return sessionFactory;
  }

  public static void shutdown() {
    // Close caches and connection pools
    getSessionFactory().close();
  }
}
```

How it works...

Here, we created the `SessionFactory` object and initialized it using the `static` block. The content inside the static block is executed only once. Here, it initializes the object of `SessionFactory` at the start of the program, and you can use it until the program's termination.

You can get the previously initially created `SessionFactory` object using the `getSessionFactory()` method. The main benefits of this method are the code's reusability and ease of use.

From now onwards for all demos, we will invoke `HibernateUtil.getSessionFactory()` method and also assume that `SessionFactory` has been successfully initialized.

The `shutdown()` method is used to close the `sessionfactory`. Once the `close()` method is invoked using the `sessionfactory` object, it close all caches and connection pools and releases all the connections to the database.

Opening a new session

A `Session` is also known as an interface that is used to get a physical connectivity with a database. It is instantiated every time we need to interact with the database for the **CRUD** (**Create, Read, Update, Delete**) operations. Persistent objects always travel from the application to the database and vice versa only through the `Session`.

Now, let's find out more about `Session` and how to open a new `Session` using a `SessionFactory`.

Getting ready

Before we create a `Session` object, we need to get an object such as a `SessionFactory` as a prerequisite:

1. Use the following code to open a new session:

```
SessionFactory sessionFactory =
HibernateUtil.getSessionFactory();
```

How to do it...

Now, we will open a new `Session` with the database:

```
Session session = sessionFactory.openSession();
```

Other methods are also available to open a `Session`, as shown in the following code:

```
Session openSession(org.hibernate.Interceptor interceptor);
Session openSession(java.sql.Connection connection,
org.hibernate.Interceptor interceptor);
```

How it works...

This will open a brand new `Session` for us. It opens the database connection when it is created and holds it until the session is closed. A `Session` created using these methods is not associated with any thread, so it's our responsibility to flush or close it once we are done with the database operation.

A `Session` is a bridge between the Java application and hibernate. The `Session` interface wraps the JDBC connection. A `Session` always tries to be in sync with the persistent store where all transactions are made.

A `Session` is always a part of first-level cache; it caches all the objects that are transmitted through that particular session. All cached objects will be destroyed once this session is closed.

Actually, opening a new `Session` for every database transaction is considered to be a good practice for a multithreaded application.

There's more...

We can use the same session instead of creating a brand-new session; hibernate provides the facility to reuse an already created session.

Let's look at how to do it:

1. Enter the following code to get the current session from `sessionFactory`:

```
SessionFactory sessionFactory =
HibernateUtil.getSessionFactory();
Session session = sessionFactory.getCurrentSession();
```

It may seem easy to get the current session, but the twist here is that you have to provide more configuration to the `Configuration` object if you plan to reuse the `Session`, as shown in the following code:

```
<property name="hibernate.current_session_context_class">
   Thread
</property>
```

In the preceding code, we set a `thread` value for the `hibernate.current_session_context_class` key, meaning that the context of the current `Session` is limited to the life of the current thread only.

For example, in a non-multithreaded environment, a `Session` is created when the main thread is started. It will close automatically once the `SessionFactory` is closed.

> This will help us more in a non-multithreaded environment because it's faster than creating a new session each time.

Opening a stateless session

Basically, a stateless session is used to perform only one task. It does not take place in any type of cache. A cache is used to store the frequently used objects in the current context. There are some cases where a stateless session is very useful; for example, if we are reading data from a file and inserting it into the database, we don't need to cache that data further because this is a one-time operation.

Apart from this, a stateless session does not use dirty checking while performing a transactional operation. The collections, as well as hibernate's event model and interceptors, are ignored by a stateless session.

How to do it...

Now, let's look at how to create a stateless session. It's the same as creating a session, but the method is different:

1. Enter the following code to open a stateless session:

```
SessionFactory sessionFactory =
HibernateUtil.getSessionFactory();
Session session = sessionFactory.openStatelessSession();
```

Saving an object to the database

Now, we have reached a point from where we start the actual transactional operations, such as insert, delete, update, and so on.

In this recipe, we will look at how to save an object to the database.

The equivalent SQL query is as follows:

▶ **Department**: INSERT INTO department (deptName) VALUES ('department name');

▶ **Employee**: INSERT INTO employee (firstName, salary, department) VALUES ('first name', salary value, department id);

How to do it...

Let's look at how to save an object to the database:

1. The following code shows how we can save an object to the database:

```
SessionFactory sessionFactory =
HibernateUtil.getSessionFactory();
Session session = sessionFactory.openSession();

// begin a transaction
session.getTransaction().begin();

//creating a department object
Department department = new Department();
department.setDeptName("developement");

// save department object
session.save(department);
System.out.println("Department saved, id:  " +
department.getId());
```

```
//creating an employee object
Employee employee = new Employee();
employee.setFirstName("yogesh");
employee.setSalary(50000);
//  set department of employee
employee.setDepartment(department);

// save employee object
session.save(employee);
System.out.println("Employee saved, id:  " +
employee.getId());

// commit transaction
session.getTransaction().commit();

session.close();
HibernateUtil.shutdown();
```

The output of the preceding code would be as follows:

```
Hibernate: insert into Department (deptName) values (?)
Department saved, id:  1
Hibernate: insert into employee (department, firstName, salary)
values (?, ?, ?)
Employee saved, id:  1
```

In the output, hibernate shows all the queries in the `values (…)` clause with the question mark (?) sign. As hibernate used `PreparedStatement` to save the record, it shows queries such as this one. If we want to see all the parameters set by hibernate, we have to configure a logging framework in our application. `Log4j` is a widely used, easy to configure, and easy to use framework.

To configure `Log4j`, we need some JAR files, which are easily available on the official site of `Log4j`, `http://logging.apache.org/log4j`.

The Maven dependency for `Log4j` is as follows:

```
<dependency>
  <groupId>log4j</groupId>
  <artifactId>log4j</artifactId>
  <version>1.2.17</version>
</dependency>
```

Also, you need to create a file with the name `log4j.properties` in your classpath. The minimal content of file should be as follows:

Source file: `Log4j.properties`

```
# Root logger option
log4j.rootLogger=INFO, stdout

# Direct log messages to stdout
log4j.appender.stdout=org.apache.log4j.ConsoleAppender
log4j.appender.stdout.Target=System.out
log4j.appender.stdout.layout=org.apache.log4j.PatternLayout

# Log JDBC bind parameter runtime arguments
log4j.logger.org.hibernate.type=trace
```

If `log4j` is configured, the output of the preceding code will be displayed as follows:

```
Hibernate: insert into Department (deptName) values (?)
binding parameter [1] as [VARCHAR] - [developement]
Department saved, id:  1
Hibernate: insert into Employee (department, firstName, salary)
values (?, ?, ?)
binding parameter [1] as [BIGINT] - [1]
binding parameter [2] as [VARCHAR] - [yogesh]
binding parameter [3] as [INTEGER] - [50000]
Employee saved, id:  1
```

In the output, you can see the logs that show all the binding parameters in sequence.

How it works...

Here, we created a department object and saved it using a `Session`. Hibernate saved the record with `id` equal to 1; even though it is not provided by us via code, once we print the value of `id` field, it shows up as 1. Actually, the `id` field is annotated with the @ `GeneratedValue` annotation, which acts as an `autoincrement` column, and the database returns a saved object back to hibernate; so, we get `id` with the value 1 here.

Perform the following steps to save the records:

1. Get the `SessionFactory`.
2. Open a new session.
3. Begin a transaction.
4. Create a department object.
5. Save a department.

6. Create an employee object.

7. Set the saved department object as an employee department.

8. Save an employee.

9. Commit the transaction.

10. Close the session.

11. Close the `SessionFactory`.

There's more...

In the preceding example, we saved the department first and then the employee. But this is just a sample case; in a working scenario, we cannot save the department every time. As we have a many-to-one relationship between department and employee, multiple employees can refer to a single department. So, we can use an already saved object, as shown in the following code:

```
SessionFactory sessionFactory = HibernateUtil.getSessionFactory();
Session session = sessionFactory.openSession();

// begin a transaction
session.getTransaction().begin();

//creating department object
Department department = new Department();
department.setId(11);

//creating an employee object
Employee employee = new Employee();
employee.setFirstName("aarush");
employee.setSalary(35000);
//  set department of employee
employee.setDepartment(department);

// save employee object
session.save(employee);
System.out.println("Employee saved, id:  " + employee.getId());

// commit transaction
session.getTransaction().commit();

session.close();
HibernateUtil.shutdown();
```

The output of the preceding code will be as follows:

```
Hibernate: insert into employee (department, firstName, salary)
values (?, ?, ?)
Employee saved, id:  2
```

 Hibernate internally creates a core SQL query with the question mark (?) sign, which is actually replaced with the value of the field by hibernate.

Here, we create the department object and set the value to 1 in the `id` field. Now, while saving an employee, hibernate sets the reference with the department having `id=1`.

 While using this method, if the object is not found in the database against the passed value, hibernate throws an error related to the violation of the foreign key constraints.

Fetching an object from the database

Now we will take a look at how to fetch objects using a `Session`. Here, we will also see how to get only one record using the primary key column. We override a `toString()` method in the `Employee` and `Department` classes so that it's easy to display the data within an object, as shown in the following code:

```
@Override
    public String toString() {
      return "\nEmployee"
      + "\n id: " + this.getId()
      + "\n first name: " + this.getFirstName()
      + "\n salary: " + this.getSalary()
      + "\n department: " + this.getDepartment().getDeptName();
    }
```

How to do it...

Here, we are trying to get an employee having `id` equals 1.

The equivalent SQL query is as follows:

```
SELECT * FROM employee WHERE id=1;
```

Now, let's look at how to do the same using hibernate:

1. Enter the following code to fetch an object of the `employee` type, where the `id` is 1:

```
SessionFactory sessionFactory =
HibernateUtil.getSessionFactory();
Session session =  sessionFactory.openSession();
Employee employee =  (Employee) session.get(Employee.class,
1l);
if(employee != null){
   System.out.println(employee.toString());
}

session.close();
HibernateUtil.shutdown();
```

The output of the preceding code will be as follows:

```
Hibernate: select employee0_.id as id0_1_, employee0_.department
as department0_1_, employee0_.firstName as firstName0_1_,
employee0_.salary as salary0_1_, department1_.id as id1_0_,
department1_.deptName as deptName1_0_ from employee employee0_
left outer join department department1_ on
employee0_.department=department1_.id where employee0_.id=?

Employee
 id: 1
 first name: yogesh
 salary: 50000.0
 department: developement
```

How it works...

Now, let's take a look at how the preceding code works. The first thing I want to highlight here is the query shown on the console/output window preceded by hibernate. Here, the hibernate engine internally creates a core SQL query to perform the operation that we can find in the console/output window. Hibernate internally uses JDBC to execute this query.

Another thing that needs to be highlighted is that we used the `Session.get(...)` method to fetch the data from the database. When you use the `Session.get(...)` method to fetch a record, it will perform the following actions:

▶ Hit the database

▶ Return a persistent instance of the given entity for the given identifier

▶ Return `null` if no record is found

It's better to check whether the object is null or not if you are using the `get()` method, because `get()` returns null if no record is found, and you will face `java.lang.NullPointerException` while accessing a null object.

There's more...

Let's consider another method named `load(...)` to fetch the data.

Now we will take a look at how to fetch data using the `load(...)` method and the difference between the `load()` and `get()` methods.

The `load()` method works in the following manner:

▶ It returns the `proxy` (hibernate term) object. This means that it returns the dummy object without hitting the database if the same object is found in a persistent state for the given identifier.

▶ If the object is not found in the session cache, it will hit the database.

▶ If no row is found in the session cache as well as in the database, then it will throw an `ObjectNotFoundException` error.

Let's take a look at some real-time scenarios.

Scenario 1

The record is in the session cache when `load()` is invoked.

Code for scenario 1

```
SessionFactory sessionFactory = HibernateUtil.getSessionFactory();
Session session = sessionFactory.openSession();
System.out.println("Employee get...");
Employee employeeGet = (Employee) session.get(Employee.class,
Long.valueOf(2));
System.out.println(employeeGet.toString());

System.out.println("Employee load...");
Employee employeeLoad = (Employee) session.load(Employee.class,Long.
valueOf(2));
System.out.println(employeeLoad.toString());

session.close();
HibernateUtil.shutdown();
```

Output for scenario 1

```
Employee get...
Hibernate: select employee0_.id as id0_1_, employee0_.department
as department0_1_, employee0_.firstName as firstName0_1_,
employee0_.salary as salary0_1_, department1_.id as id1_0_,
department1_.deptName as deptName1_0_ from employee employee0_
left outer join department department1_ on
employee0_.department=department1_.id where employee0_.id=?

Employee
 id: 2
 first name: aarush
 salary: 35000.0
 department: developement

Employee load...

Employee
 id: 2
 first name: aarush
 salary: 35000.0
 department: developement
```

Explanation for scenario 1

From the output, it's clear that when the first `get()` method is invoked, the persisted object, `Employee#2`, is stored in the session cache at that time. When `load()` is invoked, it is directly loaded from the session; there is no need to hit the database. Here, we can show that the `Select` query is executed only once.

Scenario 2

The record is not in the session cache when `load()` is invoked.

Code for scenario 2

```
SessionFactory sessionFactory = HibernateUtil.getSessionFactory();
Session session = sessionFactory.openSession();
System.out.println("Employee get...");
Employee employeeGet = (Employee) session.get(Employee.class, new
Long(1));
System.out.println(employeeGet .toString());

System.out.println("Employee load...");
Employee employeeLoad = (Employee) session.load(Employee.class,
new Long(2));
```

```
System.out.println(employeeLoad  .toString());

session.close();
HibernateUtil.shutdown();
```

Output for scenario 2

```
Employee get...
Hibernate: select employee0_.id as id0_1_, employee0_.department
as department0_1_, employee0_.firstName as firstName0_1_,
employee0_.salary as salary0_1_, department1_.id as id1_0_,
department1_.deptName as deptName1_0_ from employee employee0_
left outer join department department1_ on
employee0_.department=department1_.id where employee0_.id=?

Employee
 id: 1
 first name: yogesh
 salary: 50000.0
 department: developement

Employee load...
Hibernate: select employee0_.id as id0_1_, employee0_.department
as department0_1_, employee0_.firstName as firstName0_1_,
employee0_.salary as salary0_1_, department1_.id as id1_0_,
department1_.deptName as deptName1_0_ from employee employee0_
left outer join department department1_ on
employee0_.department=department1_.id where employee0_.id=?

Employee
 id: 2
 first name: aarush
 salary: 35000.0
 department: developement
```

Explanation for scenario 2

Here, we easily determine that when get() is invoked, it hits the database and loads Employee#1. When load() is invoked, it also hits the database, because the requested Employee#2 object is not in the session cache.

Scenario 3

The record is neither in the session cache nor in the database when load() is invoked.

Code for scenario 3

```
SessionFactory sessionFactory = HibernateUtil.getSessionFactory();
Session session = sessionFactory.openSession();
System.out.println("\nEmployee get...");
Employee employeeGet = (Employee) session.get(Employee.class, new
Long(1));
System.out.println(employeeGet.toString());

System.out.println("\nEmployee load...");
Employee employeeLoad = (Employee) session.load(Employee.class,
new Long(3));
System.out.println(employeeLoad .toString());

session.close();
HibernateUtil.shutdown();
```

Output for scenario 3

```
Employee get...
Hibernate: select employee0_.id as id0_1_, employee0_.department
as department0_1_, employee0_.firstName as firstName0_1_,
employee0_.salary as salary0_1_, department1_.id as id1_0_,
department1_.deptName as deptName1_0_ from employee employee0_
left outer join department department1_ on
employee0_.department=department1_.id where employee0_.id=?

Employee
 id: 1
 first name: yogesh
 salary: 50000.0
 department: developement

Employee load...
Hibernate: select employee0_.id as id0_1_, employee0_.department
as department0_1_, employee0_.firstName as firstName0_1_,
employee0_.salary as salary0_1_, department1_.id as id1_0_,
department1_.deptName as deptName1_0_ from employee employee0_
left outer join department department1_ on
employee0_.department=department1_.id where employee0_.id=?
Exception in thread "main" org.hibernate.ObjectNotFoundException:
No row with the given identifier exists: [vo.Employee#3]
    at
org.hibernate.impl.SessionFactoryImpl$2.handleEntityNotFound(Sessi
onFactoryImpl.java:435)
    at
org.hibernate.proxy.AbstractLazyInitializer.checkTargetState(Abstr
actLazyInitializer.java:189)
```

```
    at
org.hibernate.proxy.AbstractLazyInitializer.initialize(AbstractLaz
yInitializer.java:178)
    at
org.hibernate.proxy.AbstractLazyInitializer.getImplementation(Abst
ractLazyInitializer.java:215)
    at
org.hibernate.proxy.pojo.javassist.JavassistLazyInitializer.invoke
(JavassistLazyInitializer.java:190)
    at
vo.Employee_$$_javassist_1.getId(Employee_$$_javassist_1.java)
    at ch2.Load6.main(Load6.java:21)
```

Explanation for scenario 3

Here, `get()` hits the database and gets the `Employee#1` object. `Load` tries to find `Employee#3` in the session cache, but it will not find it there. So, it goes for the database and throws an `org.hibernate.ObjectNotFoundException` error, because `Employee#3` is not in the database either.

Removing an object from the database

Now, we take a look at how to remove a record from the database.

How to do it...

Here, we are trying to remove an `employee` object having `id` equals `1`.

The SQL query executed to achieve the same result is as follows:

```
DELETE FROM employee WHERE id=1;
```

Now, let's take a look at how to do the same using hibernate.

Code

Enter the following code to delete an object of the `employee` type, where `id` is `1`:

```
SessionFactory sessionFactory =
HibernateUtil.getSessionFactory();
Session session = sessionFactory.openSession();

session.getTransaction().begin();
Employee employee = (Employee) session.get(Employee.class,
new Long(1));
session.delete(employee);
```

```
session.getTransaction().commit();

session.close();
HibernateUtil.shutdown();
```

Output

The output will be as follows:

```
Hibernate: select employee0_.id as id0_1_, employee0_.department
as department0_1_, employee0_.firstName as firstName0_1_,
employee0_.salary as salary0_1_, department1_.id as id1_0_,
department1_.deptName as deptName1_0_ from employee employee0_
left outer join department department1_ on
employee0_.department=department1_.id where employee0_.id=?
Hibernate: delete from employee where id=?
```

How it works...

Here, the first query is executed to get the record from the database for `Employee#1`, and the second query is used to delete `Employee#1`.

The `delete(Object object)` method is void, so it returns nothing. This method throws an error if the record does not exist in the database for the given identifier.

If the record does not exist in the database, you will face the `Exception in thread "main" java.lang.IllegalArgumentException: attempt to create delete event with null entity` exception because `get()` returns the `null` object while you try to delete that object.

However, if you use the following code to delete the record, you will face another type of error:

```
Employee employee = new Employee();
employee.setId(1);
session.delete(employee);
```

When the preceding code is executed, you will face the `Exception in thread "main" org.hibernate.StaleStateException: Batch update returned unexpected row count from update [0]; actual row count: 0; expected: 1"` exception. This is because we are trying to delete `Employee#1` from the database (which does not exist), and the `employee` object is also not null; so, it throws an error.

There are many cases where you may face an exception; for example, when you try to remove a parent object that is referred to by the child object. In such cases, you will get a `foreign key constraint violated` exception.

Updating an object

Here, we look at how to get a record from the database and update the same record to the database. The main goal is to get `Employee#2` and update the first name, `aarush`, to `aarush_updated`.

How to do it...

Here, we are trying to update an `employee` object having `id` equals 2.

The SQL query executed to achieve the same result is as follows:

```
UPDATE employee SET firstName='aarush_updated' WHERE id=2;
```

Now, let's take a look at how to do the same using hibernate.

Code

Enter the following code to update an object of the `employee` type, where `id` is 2:

```
SessionFactory sessionFactory =
HibernateUtil.getSessionFactory();
Session session = sessionFactory.openSession();

/* Line 3 */ Employee employee = (Employee)
session.get(Employee.class, new Long(2));

System.out.println("\nOld Employee...");
System.out.println(employee.toString());

session.getTransaction().begin();
/* Line 9 */ employee.setFirstName("aarush_updated");
/* Line 10 */ session.update(employee);
session.getTransaction().commit();

System.out.println("\nEmployee after Update...");
System.out.println(employee.toString());

session.close();
HibernateUtil.shutdown();
```

Output

The output will be as follows:

```
Hibernate: select employee0_.id as id0_1_, employee0_.department
as department0_1_, employee0_.firstName as firstName0_1_,
employee0_.salary as salary0_1_, department1_.id as id1_0_,
department1_.deptName as deptName1_0_ from employee employee0_
left outer join department department1_ on
employee0_.department=department1_.id where employee0_.id=?

Old Employee...

Employee
 id: 2
 first name: aarush
 salary: 35000.0
 department: developement
Hibernate: update employee set department=?, firstName=?, salary=?
where id=?

Employee after Update...

Employee
 id: 2
 first name: aarush_updated
 salary: 35000.0
 department: developement
```

How it works...

Here, we used the `update()` method to update a record. The code written in the third line is used to get the particular employee for update. In the ninth line, we set a new name to the employee object and update it using the tenth line.

There's more...

In the preceding section, we used the `update()` method for updating a particular record. Apart from this method, hibernate will provide one more useful method called `saveOrUpdate()`.

This particular method is used to save or update records. Hibernate updates the records for a given object if the identifier field is given. If an identifier is not given, then hibernate will insert a new record.

Creating a criteria

Generally, we require filtered data in a SQL query, in which we use the `WHERE` clause to apply a condition to the data. Apart from the `WHERE` clause, we can use `ORDER BY` to apply sorting to the data, either ascending or descending, and `LIMIT` (if it's MySQL) to get a limited number of rows.

Hibernate allows us to perform all the operations mentioned before in an object-oriented way. A criteria is an interface; it provides an API to perform `WHERE`, `ORDER BY`, `LIMIT`, result transformation, and so on.

How to do it...

Here, we will try to create a criteria for `employee`.

The SQL query executed to achieve the same result is as follows:

```
SELECT * FROM employee;
```

Now, let's take a look at how to do the same using hibernate.

Code

Enter the following code to create a criteria for `employee`:

```
Criteria criteria = session.createCriteria(Employee.class);
List<Employee> employees = criteria.list();
for(Employee employee : employees){
System.out.println(employee.toString());
}
```

Output

The output will be as follows:

```
Hibernate: select this_.id as id0_1_, this_.department as
department0_1_, this_.firstName as firstName0_1_, this_.salary as
salary0_1_, department2_.id as id1_0_, department2_.deptName as
deptName1_0_ from employee this_ left outer join department
department2_ on this_.department=department2_.id

Employee
 id: 1
 first name: yogesh
 salary: 50000.0
 department: developement
```

```
Employee
  id: 2
  first name: aarush_updated
  salary: 35000.0
  department: developement
```

How it works...

Here, we created a criteria for the `Employee` class, and using it, we tried to load all the records from the `Employee` table. Previously, we used `session.load()` or `session.get()` to fetch the record from the database, but these methods return only one record at a time. Now, we can fetch multiple records using `criteria()`.

The `criteria.list()` method returns `java.util.List<Object>`. In our example it returns `java.util.List<Employee>` because we created a criteria using the `Employee` class.

Restricting the results using a criteria

Let's take a look at how to add restrictions, which are equal to the `WHERE` clause in SQL.

How to do it...

Let's consider that we have four records in the employee table, as shown in the following tables:

This is the `Employee` table:

department	salary	firstName	id
1	50000	Yogesh	1
1	35000	Aarush	2
3	30000	Varsha	3
2	75000	Vishal	4

This is the `Department` table:

deptName	id
development	1
R&D	2
UI/UX	3

Now, the scenario is that we want to get only those employees whose salary is greater than `35000`.

The equivalent SQL query to select the above employees is as follows:

```
SELECT * FROM employee WHERE salary > 35000;
```

Now, let's look at how to do the same using hibernate.

Code

Enter the following code to create a criteria for `employee`:

```
Criteria criteria = session.createCriteria(Employee.class);
criteria.add(Restrictions.gt("salary", 35000));
List<Employee> employees = criteria.list();
for (Employee employee : employees) {
    System.out.println(employee.toString());
}
```

Output

The output will be as follows:

```
Hibernate: select this_.id as id0_1_, this_.department as
department0_1_, this_.firstName as firstName0_1_, this_.salary as
salary0_1_, department2_.id as id1_0_, department2_.deptName as
deptName1_0_ from employee this_ left outer join department
department2_ on this_.department=department2_.id where
this_.salary>?

Employee
 id: 1
 first name: yogesh
 salary: 50000.0
 department: developement

Employee
 id: 6
 first name: vishal
 salary: 75000.0
 department: R&D
```

How it works...

Here, you need to understand the line `criteria.add(Restrictions.gt("salary", 35000d));` only.

We represent `WHERE salary > 35000` in `Restrictions.gt("salary", 35000d)`, **gt**, that is, using the *greater than* sign. It will find all the records of the employees having a salary greater than `35000`.

There are many functions available in the class `Restrictions`. You can use logical operators such as:

- gt(>, greater than)
- ge(>=, greater than or equal to)
- lt(<, less than)
- le(<=, less than or equal to)
- eq(=, equal to)
- ne(<>, !=, not equal to)

Apart from these logical operators, you can use:

- like (to perform Like operation)
- iLike (to perform Like operation with ignore case)
- Not
- Between
- In
- Or
- isNull
- isNotNull
- isEmpty
- isNotEmpty, and many more useful functions

These will help us to represent the SQL expression in hibernate notation.

We can add multiple conditions by adding more `criteria.add()` statements.

 Remember that when you add more restrictions using the `criteria.add()` method, hibernate considers the AND (&&) condition between all restriction conditions.

Pagination using a criteria

Now we will look at how to limit the number of rows using hibernate.

How to do it...

Here's a scenario to easily understand what we are about to do.

Let's consider that we have four rows in an employee table, and a `SELECT * FROM employee` SQL query returns all four records. However, if we want only the second and third records, we can use the `SELECT * FROM employee LIMIT 1, 2` SQL statement.

Let's take a look at how to achieve such a condition in hibernate:

Code

Enter the following code to paginate using a criteria:

```
SessionFactory sessionFactory =
HibernateUtil.getSessionFactory();
Session session = sessionFactory.openSession();

Criteria criteria = session.createCriteria(Employee.class);
criteria.setFirstResult(1); // represent LIMIT 1,* in MySQL
criteria.setMaxResults(2);// represent LIMIT *,2 in MySQL

List<Employee> employees = criteria.list();
for (Employee employee : employees) {
  System.out.println(employee.toString());
}

session.close();
HibernateUtil.shutdown();
```

Output

The output will be as follows:

```
Hibernate: select this_.id as id0_1_, this_.department as
department0_1_, this_.firstName as firstName0_1_, this_.salary as
salary0_1_, department2_.id as id1_0_, department2_.deptName as
deptName1_0_ from employee this_ left outer join department
department2_ on this_.department=department2_.id limit ?, ?

Employee
  id: 2
```

```
     first name: aarush
     salary: 35000.0
     department: developement

  Employee
    id: 3
    first name: varsha
    salary: 30000.0
    department: UI/UX
```

You can use pagination and restrictions together as well.

How it works...

Here, two methods play a main role: the first is `setFirstResult()` and the second is `setMaxResult()`. The `setFirstResult()` method is used to set a start limit, and `setMaxResult()` is used to set the maximum limit. Hibernate adds the database-dependent clause; for example, hibernate adds the `LIMIT` clause here as the current database is MySQL.

Sorting the results

In SQL, we use the `ORDER BY` clause to sort a result by column name and either ascending or descending order. We can achieve the same thing in hibernate as well.

How to do it...

Let's suppose that we selected all the records from the employee table, and then, by default, the records were sorted by the primary key column. But now, we want all the records to be sorted by the descending order of `firstName`.

Now, the scenario is to select all the employees and order them using their first name.

The equivalent SQL query to do this is is as follows:

```
SELECT * FROM employee ORDER BY firstName DESC;
```

Consider the following table data for this recipe:

department	salary	firstName	id
1	50000	Yogesh	1
1	35000	Aarush	2
3	30000	Varsha	3
2	75000	Vishal	4

Let's take a look at how to achieve such a condition in hibernate:

Code

Enter the following code to sort the results according to the employee's first name:

```
Criteria criteria = session.createCriteria(Employee.class);
criteria.addOrder(Order.desc("firstName")); // desc() used to add
order Descending
// criteria.addOrder(Order.asc("id")); // asc() used to add order
Ascending

List<Employee> employees = criteria.list();
for (Employee employee : employees) {
  System.out.println(employee.toString());
}
```

Output

```
Hibernate: select this_.id as id1_1_1_, this_.department_id as
departme4_1_1_, this_.firstName as firstNam2_1_1_, this_.salary as
salary3_1_1_, department2_.id as id1_0_0_, department2_.deptName
as deptName2_0_0_ from Employee this_ left outer join Department
department2_ on this_.department_id=department2_.id order by
this_.firstName desc

Employee
 id: 1
 first name: Yogesh
 salary: 50000
 department: development

Employee
 id: 4
 first name: Vishal
 salary: 75000
 department: R&D

Employee
 id: 3
 first name: Varsha
 salary: 30000
 department: UI/UX

Employee
 id: 2
```

```
first name: Aarush
salary: 35000
department: development
```

How it works...

In a general scenario, when the ORDER BY clause is not supplied, the database returns records in the default order in which data is stored.

Here, we applied the descending order to the firstName column, so the employee Yogesh comes first, and Aarush goes last. The order by this_.firstName desc clause is used by hibernate to get the desired results.

Transforming a result

As a developer, I love this feature, as it helps the developers to transform the returned rows to List, Map, or user-defined Bean.

How to do it...

Now we will take a look at three scenarios of the demonstration code that will convert the records returned by hibernate to List, Map, and Bean.

Here, we use the Transformers class to provide the transforming mechanism to criteria.

Scenario 1: Converting a result to List

All the demos up to this point show that if we use the criteria.list() method, the resultant data is always returned in List. However, you can still use Transformers.TO_LIST in criteria, as follows:

```
criteria.setResultTransformer(Transformers.TO_LIST);
```

This means that every row in the result will be represented as a List.

Scenario 2: Converting a result to Map

Now, let's see how to convert the resultant data in Map:

```
criteria.setResultTransformer(Transformers.ALIAS_TO_ENTITY_MAP);
```

This means every object from List represents Map.

Code

For example, the following code shows how to transform the resultant data into `Map`:

```
Criteria criteria = session.createCriteria(Employee.class);
criteria.setResultTransformer(Transformers.ALIAS_TO_ENTITY_MAP);
List list = criteria.list();
System.out.println("List: " + list);
Map map = (Map) list.get(0);
Employee employeeMap = (Employee) map.get(Criteria.ROOT_ALIAS);
System.out.println(employeeMap.toString());
```

Output

The output will be as follows:

```
List: [{this=Employee@3235025a}, {this=Employee@4e84c320},
{this=Employee@2644f3a2}, {this=Employee@7c7d8dfe}]
Employee
 id: 2
 first name: aarush
 salary: 35000.0
 department: developement
```

When we print out a list object in the console, we can see that it's represented as key and value format in the `Map` structure. We will try to get the value from `map` at the zero position using the following code:

```
Map map = (Map) list.get(0);
```

The key of `Map` is `this`, and the value is the object of the `Employee` class.

So, the standard way to access a map's value is by its key. Here, the key is `this`, which is the equivalent of the `Root` alias of `criteria` in hibernate. So, you can access an object of `Employee` with the help of the following code:

```
Employee employeeMap = (Employee) map.get(Criteria.ROOT_ALIAS);
```

Scenario 3: Converting a result to user-defined Bean

This feature is useful when we select the columns in the resultant data and want to form that data in an already defined `Bean`.

For example, if we select the `empId`, `empFirstName`, `empSalary`, and the `empDeptName`, we can easily form this data into an `EmployeeDetail` bean, as we already have a bean defined with the name `EmployeeDetail.java` with these four fields:

```
public class EmployeeDetail {
    private long empId;
    private String empFirstName;
```

```java
    private double empSalary;
    private String empDeptName;

    public long getEmpId() {
      return empId;
    }

    public void setEmpId(long empId) {
      this.empId = empId;
    }

    public String getEmpFirstName() {
      return empFirstName;
    }

    public void setEmpFirstName(String empFirstName) {
      this.empFirstName = empFirstName;
    }

    public double getEmpSalary() {
      return empSalary;
    }

    public void setEmpSalary(double empSalary) {
      this.empSalary = empSalary;
    }

    public String getEmpDeptName() {
      return empDeptName;
    }

    public void setEmpDeptName(String empDeptName) {
      this.empDeptName = empDeptName;
    }

    @Override
    public String toString() {
      return "\nEmployeeDetail "
          + "\n Employee id: " + this.empId
          + "\n Employee FirstName: " + this.empFirstName
          + "\n Employee Salary: " + this.empSalary
          + "\n Employee DepartmentName : " + this.empDeptName;
    }

}
```

Code

Now, the following code shows how to convert the resultant data into an `EmployeeDetail` bean:

```
Criteria criteria = session.createCriteria(Employee.class);
criteria.createAlias("department", "_department");

ProjectionList projectionList = Projections.projectionList();
projectionList.add(Projections.alias(Projections.property("id"),
"empId"));
projectionList.add(Projections.alias(Projections.property("firstNa
me"), "empFirstName"));
projectionList.add(Projections.alias(Projections.property("salary"
), "empSalary"));
projectionList.add(Projections.alias(Projections.property("_depart
ment.deptName"), "empDeptName"));
criteria.setProjection(projectionList);

criteria.setResultTransformer(Transformers.aliasToBean(EmployeeDet
ail.class));
List<EmployeeDetail> employeeDetails = criteria.list();

EmployeeDetail employeeDetail = employeeDetails.get(0);
System.out.println(employeeDetail.toString());
```

Output

The output will be as follows:

```
EmployeeDetail
  Employee id: 1
  Employee FirstName: yogesh
  Employee Salary: 50000.0
  Employee DepartmentName : developement
```

To use this feature in hibernate, we need to match a resultant column alias with a fieldname in the bean. For example, here we gave `empId` as an alias of the `id` field.

Actually, here you will notice a new term known as projection, which we will discuss in the next section.

Using basic projection

First of all, let's understand what projection is. It is a class provided by hibernate that is used to select a particular field while querying. Apart from that, we can use some built-in aggregation functions provided by hibernate.

Here, we will only consider a basic projection. Now, the scenario is that we need only the `id` and `firstName` fields from the `employee` table to set them in projection.

If we have only one field to select, we can directly use the following code:

```
setProjection(Projections object);
```

However, if we need more than one column in the result, we need to use the `ProjectionList` class, as follows:

```
setProjection(ProjectionList object);
```

When we use `ProjectionList`, hibernate returns `List<Object>` in the result. So, it's better to use `ALIAS_TO_ENTITY_MAP` for the ease of access of fields; however, it depends on the actual requirement.

How to do it...

Here, we will take a look at two scenarios that show how to select single and multiple fields while querying with hibernate.

Scenario 1:

We want to select only one field using.

The equivalent SQL query to select only the `id` column from the `employee` table is as follows:

SELECT id FROM employee.

Let's take a look at how to achieve such a condition in hibernate:

Code

Enter the following code:

```
Criteria criteria = session.createCriteria(Employee.class);
criteria.setProjection(Projections.property("id"));
System.out.println(criteria.list());
```

Output

The output will be as follows:

```
Hibernate: select this_.id as y0_ from employee this_
[1, 2, 3, 4]
```

Scenario 2:

We want to select multiple fields.

The equivalent SQL query to select multiple `id` and `firstName` columns from the `employee` table in hibernate is as follows:

```
SELECT id, firstName FROM employee.
```

Let's take a look at how to achieve such a condition in hibernate:

Code

Enter the following code:

```
Criteria criteria = session.createCriteria(Employee.class);
ProjectionList projectionList =
Projections.projectionList();
projectionList.add(Projections.alias(Projections.property("
id"), "empId"));
projectionList.add(Projections.alias(Projections.property("
firstName"), "empFirstName"));
criteria.setProjection(projectionList);
criteria.setResultTransformer(Transformers.ALIAS_TO_ENTITY_
MAP);
List list = criteria.list();
System.out.println(list);
```

Output

The output will be as follows:

```
[{empId=1, empFirstName=yogesh}, {empId=2, empFirstName=aarush},
{empId=3, empFirstName=varsha}, {empId=4, empFirstName=vishal}]
```

From the output, we can easily determine that projection is applied and only the two required columns are returned.

Now you will easily understand how projection works.

3
Basic Annotations

In this chapter, we will cover the following recipes:

- Declaring a class as an entity and creating a table in the database – `@Entity` and `@Table`
- Creating a column in the table – `@Column`
- Creating a primary key and composite primary key column – `@Id` and `@IdClass`
- Creating an `autogenerator` column

Introduction

Annotation is used to provide a metadata of code. It is a part of the code file itself. It is used to give some extra information about the code and can be used with variables, method packages, the interface, or the class itself.

The advantages of annotation are that it's easy to use and makes the development process faster. Before annotation was introduced, there were many methodologies which were used to provide information to the code, such as XML-based mapping. Here, we will take a look at how annotations are useful in the development process.

In this chapter, we will consider the basic and necessary annotations used to start development using hibernate.

Declaring a class as an entity and creating a table in the database – @Entity and @Table

We need a class to be declared as an entity for hibernate to use it. Hibernate considers the class as a persistent class if it is annotated with the `@Entity` annotation.

How to do it...

Perform the following steps to declare a class as a hibernate entity:

1. Enter the following code on your editor:

```
@Entity
public class Employee {
    // Fields and getter/setter
}
```

Here, we annotate a class, `Employee`, with the `@Entity` annotation. As a result, hibernate considers the current class eligible to be persisted.

> If you build a session factory with the preceding code and the table name is not given, hibernate will create a table with the name `employee`, which is equal to the class name.

2. If we want a user-defined table name rather than a default name, we can use the `@Table` annotation. The following code shows us how to achieve this:

```
@Entity
@Table(name="tbl_employee")
public class Employee {
    // Fields and getter/setter
}
```

Here, we give `name="tbl_employee"` as a parameter in the `@Table` annotation. So, hibernate will override the default table name with the name `"tbl_employee"`.

There is another attribute available with `@Table` annotations; let's take a look at it.

This attribute is called `uniqueConstraints`. It is used when we need the `UNIQUE` key constraint with multiple fields.

The following code shows how to do this:

```
@Entity
@Table(name = "tbl_employee", uniqueConstraints =
@UniqueConstraint(columnNames = { "id" , "empCode"}))
```

```
public class Employee {

    @Id
    private long id;

    @Column
    private String empCode;

    // Fields and getter/setter

}
```

When a `SessionFactory` is created for the first time and property `hbm2ddl.auto` is set to `create`, hibernate will execute the following queries to create a table and the unique key constraints:

```
Hibernate: drop table if exists tbl_employee
Hibernate: create table tbl_employee (id bigint not null, empCode
varchar(255), primary key (id))
Hibernate: alter table tbl_employee add constraint
UK_3r763mmnyundobvaiqjv6lnj1  unique (id, empCode)
```

When the table is created using the preceding code, hibernate will create the UNIQUE key using two fields: id and empCode.

Take a look at the following script belonging to the table created by hibernate to understand `uniqueConstraints`:

```
CREATE TABLE `tbl_employee` (
  `id` bigint(20) NOT NULL,
  `empCode` varchar(255) DEFAULT NULL,
  PRIMARY KEY (`id`),
  UNIQUE KEY `id` (`id`,`empCode`)
);
```

 The `uniqueConstraints` is useful when we need a UNIQUE constraint for multiple fields. For only one column, you can use the `@Column(unique=true)` annotation directly on the field.

How it works...

Hibernate uses the declared annotation at the time of compilation to get the information applied to the Java code. You can't persist a class if it is not annotated with `@Entity` or defined in `*.hbm.xml`.

The `@Table` annotation is an optional annotation and is used when the custom table name is required.

Creating a column in the table – @Column

In the previous recipe, you learned how to create a table in the database with attributes. Now, we will take a look at how to declare a column in the table with some useful options.

How to do it...

First of all, we take a basic example of creating a column:

1. We will first create a column with the name `empCode` in the `employee` table. As no information is provided for the column name, hibernate uses a variable name. Enter the following code:

```
@Entity
public class Employee {
    @Column
    private String empCode;

    // fields and getter/setter

}
```

2. If we need a custom column name, we can use the name attribute, as shown in the following code:

```
@Column(name="emp_code")
private String empCode;
```

Now, hibernate will create a column with the name `"emp_code"`.

There's more...

Let's take a look at some useful attributes available for the `@Column` annotation.

length

The `length` attribute is used to provide the column with a maximum size.

Here is an example:

```
@Column(name="emp_code", length=100)
private String empCode;
```

 If `length` is not provided, the default size of the data type is used, and it is database-specific.

nullable

The `nullable` attribute accepts a Boolean value. If `nullable` is `true`, it means that the column contains a NULL value. It does not accept NULL if the value of `nullable` is set to `false`, but the default value of `nullable` is `true`.

Here is an example:

```
@Column(name="emp_code", nullable=false)
private String empCode;
```

unique

The `unique` attribute also accepts a Boolean value. If `unique` is set to `true`, hibernate will create a column with a UNIQUE index. However, the default value is `false`.

Here is an example:

```
@Column(name="emp_code", unique=true)
private String empCode;
```

Here, hibernate creates a UNIQUE index for the `"emp_code"` column.

columnDefinition

This is a useful attribute of the annotation. It accepts a string value. We can give it a SQL fragment, which is used at the time of table creation.

Let's consider a useful example.

If we have a date field and want to set a default date but no date is provided at the time of the insertion of the rows, we can use the following code:

```
@Column(columnDefinition = "timestamp NOT NULL DEFAULT
CURRENT_TIMESTAMP")
private Date startDate;
```

Hibernate directly uses this string while creating the table.

scale and precision

We will consider scale and precision together for a better understanding.

The `precision` and `scale` attributes come into the picture when we have the decimal data type of the column and want to store the value with the decimal point.

Here is an example:

```
@Column(precision = 7, scale = 2)
private BigDecimal salary;
```

This will create a salary column with the decimal data type and length 7, 2. This means that you can enter a value up to 7 and from among that 2 digit contains decimal part.

insertable and updatable

Both these attributes accept a Boolean value. This denotes whether the column takes part in the insert and update operations or not.

See also...

There is another annotation, @JoinColumn, which is used when we want a reference between tables. We will discuss this is in *Chapter 5, Working with Associations*.

Creating a primary key and composite primary key column – @Id and @IdClass

It's necessary to declare an Identity column in each class while developing with hibernate. Sometimes, when we need to declare a primary key as a combination of multiple columns, we call this the *composite* primary key, as the primary key is composed of multiple columns. We can declare a column with the primary key constraint and also generate a composite primary key using hibernate.

How to do it...

Let's start with a primary key declaration:

1. To declare a column as a primary key column, we use the @Id annotation, as follows:

```
@Id
private long id;
```

When the preceding code is executed, hibernate creates a column with the name id and also adds the primary key index to it. In this case, @Column is not required unless you want a custom column name.

2. To declare it as a composite primary key, we will consider creating a composite primary key using the employee's first name and phone. Therefore, the firstName column will be duplicated, but the combination of both the firstName and phone column will never be duplicated. Let's take a look at how to achieve this by coding:

```
@Entity
@IdClass(Employee.class)
public class Employee implements Serializable {
  @Id
  private String firstName;
```

```
    @Id
    private String phone;
  }
```

Here, we annotated the `firstName` and `phone` columns with `@Id`, which means that we want to create a primary key for both. Also, we annotated the entity class with the `@IdClass` annotation.

 Another thing that needs to be taken care of is that the entity class must implement `Serializable` if you plan to store the entity in any cache, session, or you wish to transfer the entity over wire. It is not necessary, but recommended.

The following table script shows how the composite primary key is generated:

```
CREATE TABLE `employee` (
  `phone` varchar(255) NOT NULL,
  `firstName` varchar(255) NOT NULL,
  PRIMARY KEY (`phone`,`firstName`)
);
```

Creating an autogenerator column

Generally, we create a primary column with some autogenerated value. Hibernate allows us to create the same using code. Let's take a look at some methods to create a column with an autogenerated value.

How to do it...

We can create an autogenerated column in many ways, such as:

- Using a default generation strategy
- Using a sequence generator
- Using a table generator

Default generation strategy

To use a default strategy for autogeneration, we will use the `@GeneratedValue` annotation, as follows:

```
@Id
@GeneratedValue
private long id;
```

Using the preceding code, hibernate will create a column with an autoincremental value.

By default, hibernate uses the `GenerationType.AUTO` strategy if no strategy is supplied; so, `@GeneratedValue` is equal to `@GeneratedValue(strategy=GenerationType.AUTO)`.

Still, as it is database-specific, it's the responsibility of the database to provide a value for this column, and the same rule is applied for `@GeneratedValue(strategy=GenerationType.IDENTITY)`.

Sequence generator

Here, we are using `GenerationType.SEQUENCE` in the `@GeneratedValue` annotation; let's take a look at how to do it.

Generally, the value for the column is provided by the database if it is a sequence.

We can create a sequence in the database, if it is supported by the database, and add the mapping in the Java code, as shown in the following code.

For example, our database sequence is created with the name `"seq"`. We can use the same, as shown in the following code:

```
@Id
@SequenceGenerator(name="seq", sequenceName="DB_SEQ")
@GeneratedValue(strategy=GenerationType.SEQUENCE, generator="seq")
private long id;
```

Here, the `sequenceName = "DB_SEQ"` value is a sequence name in the database, which is manually created by us.

Table generator

In a table generator, the value for the primary key column is stored in one table. Hibernate uses this table to get the next value for the primary key column in the particular class.

Let's take a look at how to do it using code:

```
@Id
@Column(name = "id")
@GeneratedValue(strategy = GenerationType.TABLE, generator =
"gen_tbl")
@TableGenerator(name = "gen_tbl", table = "gen_table", pkColumnName
= "pk", valueColumnName = "id", pkColumnValue = "employee0",
initialValue = 0, allocationSize = 1)
private long id;
```

Here, we used the `@TableGenerator` annotation to define a table generator.

There's more...

Let's take a look at some attributes available in the `@GeneratedValue` and `@Table Generator` annotations.

Attributes available in the @GeneratedValue annotation

Let's consider some attributes available in the `@GeneratedValue` annotation.

Strategy

This attribute accepts the `enum GenerationType` value.

Four possible values available for `enum GenerationType` are as follows:

- AUTO
- IDENTITY
- SEQUENCE
- TABLE

Generator

This attribute accepts a string value; it's the name of the generator in `GenerationType.SEQUENCE` and `GenerationType.TABLE`.

Attributes available in @TableGenerator annotation

Now, we will consider some attributes of `@TableGenerator`.

name

The `name` attribute accepts a string value and defines a unique name for the table generator in a class. It is used in the `@GeneratedValue` annotation to provide a value to the generator attribute.

Here is an example:

```
name = "gen_tbl"
```

table

The `table` attribute accepts a string value. It is a new table name created by hibernate to contain the next value for the primary key column.

Here is an example:

```
table = "gen_table"
```

Here, hibernate will create a table with the name `"gen_table"`.

pkColumnName

This attribute accepts a string value. It defines a column with the name `"gen_table"` in the table to store a key for the class.

Here is an example:

```
pkColumnName = "pk"
```

Here, hibernate will create a column with the name `"pk"` in the `"gen_table"` table.

valueColumnName

This attribute accepts a string value. It is another column used by hibernate to hold an actual value for the primary key column.

Here is an example:

```
valueColumnName = "id"
```

Here, hibernate will create a column with the name `"id"` in the `"gen_table"` table.

pkColumnValue

This is a static value for the particular class stored in the `"pk"` column. It is used to get a value for the primary key, which is stored in the `"id"` column against this value.

Here is an example:

```
pkColumnValue = "employee"
```

Here, hibernate will insert a row in `"gen_table"` with the `"employee"` value in the `"pk"` column and provide a value in the `"id"` column, which is equal to `initialValue`.

initialValue

This attribute defines an initial value for the primary column.

Here is an example:

```
initialValue = 0
```

allocationSize

This attribute defines the increment in a value for the primary key column.

Here is an example:

```
allocationSize = 1
```

Once the code is executed, hibernate will create the following table structure in the database:

Table: `employee`

id
1

Table: `gen_table`

pk	id
Employee	2

Here, the `"gen_table"` table shows a value in `"id"`, which is 2, because we inserted a 1 record in `employee`, then hibernate updated the value of the `"id"` column for the `"employee"` key by `allocationSize` (here value 1).

4
Working with Collections

In this chapter, we will cover the following recipes:

- ▶ Persisting `List`
- ▶ Persisting `Set`
- ▶ Persisting `Map`
- ▶ Persisting `Array`

Introduction

Hibernate allows us to map the Java collections object with data structures. In this chapter, we will look at how to deal with Java collections using Hibernate. Java collections commonly include `List`, `Map`, `Set`, and `Array`. All standard Java collections are supported by hibernate.

Persisting List

`List` is an interface provided by Java and accessed from `java.util.List` that has the capability to store a sequence of elements, allow duplicate elements, and contain elements of the same type. Some classes that implement the `List` interface are `java.util.ArrayList`, `java.util.LinkedList`, and so on. Now, let's look at how to use `List` while using hibernate.

Getting ready

Here, we consider a new table structure for `employee`, and each employee has multiple e-mail addresses. So, we create an `Employee` class that has the `List<String>` field e-mails called list of e-mail addresses. Here, we use the `List` class for this recipe. To achieve this, we need to create classes and tables; so, first of all, let's meet the basic prerequisites.

Creating tables

Use the following script to create the tables, unless you are using `hbm2dll=create|update` to dynamically create the table using hibernate.

Use the following code to create the `employee` table:

```
CREATE TABLE `employee` (
  `id` BIGINT(20) NOT NULL AUTO_INCREMENT,
  `name` VARCHAR(255) DEFAULT NULL,
  PRIMARY KEY (`id`)
);
```

Use the following code to create the `email` table:

```
CREATE TABLE `email` (
  `Employee_id` BIGINT(20) NOT NULL,
  `emails` VARCHAR(255) DEFAULT NULL,
  `email_index` INT(11) NOT NULL,
  PRIMARY KEY (`Employee_id`,`email_index`),
  KEY `FK5C24B9C37808516` (`Employee_id`),
  CONSTRAINT `FK5C24B9C37808516` FOREIGN KEY (`Employee_id`)
  REFERENCES `employee` (`id`)
);
```

Creating a class

Use the following code to create a class:

Source file: `Employee.java`

```
@Entity
@Table(name = "employee")
public class Employee {

    @Id
    @GeneratedValue
    @Column(name = "id")
    private long id;
```

```java
@Column(name = "name")
private String name;

@ElementCollection(fetch=FetchType.LAZY)
@CollectionTable(name = "email")
@IndexColumn(name="email_index")
private List<String> emails;

public long getId() {
  return id;
}

public void setId(long id) {
  this.id = id;
}

public String getName() {
  return name;
}

public void setName(String name) {
  this.name = name;
}

public List<String> getEmails() {
  return emails;
}

public void setEmails(List<String> emails) {
  this.emails = emails;
}

@Override
public String toString() {
  return "Employee"
      + "\n\tId:" + this.id
      + "\n\tName:" + this.name
      + "\n\tEmails:" + this.emails;
}

}
```

How to do it...

In this section, we will take a look at how to insert, retrieve, delete, and update List, step by step.

Inserting a record

The following code is used to insert a record into the database. Here, we will try to insert the record of an employee with three e-mail addresses:

Code

```
    SessionFactory sessionFactory =
HibernateUtil.getSessionFactory();
    Session session = sessionFactory.openSession();

    Employee employee = new Employee();
    employee.setName("yogesh");

    List<String> emails = new ArrayList<String>();
    emails.add("emailaddress1@provider1.com");
    emails.add("emailaddress2@provider2.com");
    emails.add("emailaddress3@provider3.com");
    employee.setEmails(emails);

    session.getTransaction().begin();
    session.save(employee);
    session.getTransaction().commit();
```

Output

```
Hibernate: insert into employee (name) values (?)
Hibernate: insert into email (Employee_id, email_index, emails)
values (?,?,?)
Hibernate: insert into email (Employee_id, email_index, emails)
values (?,?,?)
Hibernate: insert into email (Employee_id, email_index, emails)
values (?,?,?)
Employee
  Id: 1
  Name: yogesh
  Emails: [emailaddress1@provider1.com,
emailaddress2@provider2.com, emailaddress3@provider3.com]
```

When this code is executed, it inserts one record into the employee table and three into the email table. It also sets a primary key value for the employee record in each record of the email table as a reference.

Retrieving a record

Here, we know that the record is inserted with id 1. So, we will try to get only this record and understand how `List` works.

Use the following code to retrieve the records of `Employee#1`:

Code

```
Employee employee = (Employee) session.get(Employee.class, 1l);
System.out.println(employee.toString());
```

Output

```
Hibernate: select employee0_.id as id0_0_, employee0_.name as
name0_0_ from employee employee0_ where employee0_.id=?
Hibernate: select emails0_.Employee_id as Employee1_0_0_,
emails0_.emails as emails0_, emails0_.email_index as email3_0_
from email emails0_ where emails0_.Employee_id=?
Employee
  Id: 1
  Name: yogesh
  Emails: [emailaddress1@provider1.com,
emailaddress2@provider2.com, emailaddress3@provider3.com]
```

Here, we notice that hibernate executes two different queries: one is to load the `employee` object and the other to load all the e-mail addresses referenced to that particular employee.

Updating a record

Here, we will try to add one more e-mail address to the list of e-mail IDs for `Employee#1`, which means that we will update the list of e-mails. Use the following code to do so:

Code

```
Employee employee = (Employee) session.get(Employee.class, 1l);
List<String> emails = employee.getEmails();
emails.add("emailaddress3@provider3.com");
session.getTransaction().begin();
session.saveOrUpdate(employee);
session.getTransaction().commit();
 System.out.println(employee.toString());
```

Output

```
Hibernate: select employee0_.id as id0_0_, employee0_.name as
name0_0_ from employee employee0_ where employee0_.id=?
Hibernate: select emails0_.Employee_id as Employee1_0_0_,
emails0_.emails as emails0_, emails0_.email_index as email3_0_
from email emails0_ where emails0_.Employee_id=?
```

```
Hibernate: insert into email (Employee_id, email_index, emails)
values (?,?,?)
Employee
  Id: 1
  Name: yogesh
  Emails: [emailaddress1@provider1.com,
emailaddress2@provider2.com, emailaddress3@provider3.com,
emailaddress3@provider3.com]
```

Here, we can see that we have two e-mail addresses with the same value, `emailaddress3@provider3.com`. This happens because here we used `List`, and it allows the existence of duplicate elements.

Deleting a record

Here, we will try to delete the record of `Employee#1` from the database using the following code:

Code

```
Employee employee = new Employee();
employee.setId(1);
session.getTransaction().begin();
session.delete(employee);
session.getTransaction().commit();
```

Output

```
Hibernate: delete from email where Employee_id=?
Hibernate: delete from employee where id=?
```

While deleting the employee record, hibernate also deletes all the child records associated with `Employee#1`; in our case, these are the e-mail addresses.

How it works...

When we use `hbm2dll=auto|update`, hibernate will create two tables for us: one is `employee` and the other is `email`:

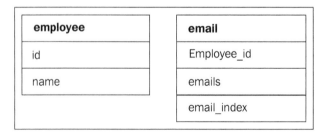

employee	email
id	Employee_id
name	emails
	email_index

An important point that needs to be highlighted here is as follows:

```
@ElementCollection(fetch=FetchType.LAZY)
@CollectionTable(name = "email")
@IndexColumn(name="email_index")
private List<String> emails;
```

Let's take a look at the preceding code in detail:

▸ @CollectionTable: This annotation indicates that the current field is of the Collection type, and hibernate creates a separate table for it. It also creates a reference between them. In this case, hibernate creates a table named email with email and employee_id. The employee_id column is made by joining the persisted class name and the primary key column of the employee class with an underscore (_).

▸ @ElementCollection: This annotation is used to define the relationship with the embedded or basic type.

Here, we also use the fetch=FetchType.LAZY attribute, which means that hibernate will load a child or referenced record on demand only. In our *Retrieving a record* example, it will execute the employee and e-mail queries separately. Hibernate uses FetchType.LAZY if no attribute is defined for fetch.

Another possible value with the fetch attribute is FetchType.EAGER, which means that hibernate will load all the child records at the time of the retrieval of the parent record. In other words, it eagerly loads all the records. If we use FetchType.EAGER, hibernate uses the following query:

```
Hibernate:
SELECT
  employee0_.id AS id0_0_,
  employee0_.name AS name0_0_,
  emails1_.Employee_id AS Employee1_0_2_,
  emails1_.emails AS emails2_,
  emails1_.email_index AS email3_2_
FROM
  employee employee0_
  LEFT OUTER JOIN email emails1_
    ON employee0_.id = emails1_.Employee_id
WHERE employee0_.id = ?
```

The preceding code uses left outer join to get the child records, the reason being that when we use FetchType.LAZY, hibernate executes a separate query to load the child or referenced record.

If we use FetchType.EAGER, hibernate will use the JOIN query to get the child records.

Here, hibernate uses the left outer join to get child records, because `FetchType.EAGER` is used in the code.

```
@IndexColumn(name="email_index")
```

This annotation is used to hold the indexes of the collection's elements. This means that Hibernate creates a separate column in the child table (here, `email`) with the value given in the attribute name (here, `email_index`). This column preserves the sequence of the collection objects and helps while retrieving the records.

There's more...

In the preceding example, we dealt with `List` of the basic data type, which means that we used `List` of `String` (`List<String>`). Now, let's consider that we have a `Degree` class, which contains the degree name and passing year and want to map it with `Employee`. For this, we deal with `List<Object>` instead of `List<String>`. In our case, it will be `List<Degree>`. Let's take a look at how to do it.

Creating classes

Use the following code to create the classes:

Source file: `Degree.java`

```java
@Entity
@Table(name="degree")
public class Degree {

  @Id
  @GeneratedValue
  private long id;

  @Column(name="degreename")
  private String degreeName;

  @Column(name="passingyear")
  private int passingYear;

  public Degree() {

  }

  public Degree(String degreeName, int passingYear) {
    this.degreeName = degreeName;
    this.passingYear = passingYear;
  }
```

```
      public long getId() {
        return id;
      }

      public void setId(long id) {
        this.id = id;
      }

      public String getDegreeName() {
        return degreeName;
      }

      public void setDegreeName(String degreeName) {
        this.degreeName = degreeName;
      }

      public int getPassingYear() {
        return passingYear;
      }

      public void setPassingYear(int passingYear) {
        this.passingYear = passingYear;
      }

      @Override
      public String toString() {
        return "\n\nDegree "
            + "\n\tId:" + this.id
            + "\n\tName:" + this.degreeName
            + "\n\tPassing year:" + this.passingYear;
      }
    }
```

Source file: `Employee.java`

```
    @Entity
    @Table(name = "employee")
    public class Employee {

      @Id
      @GeneratedValue
      @Column(name = "id")
      private long id;

      @Column(name = "name")
      private String name;
```

```
@OneToMany(cascade={CascadeType.ALL})
private List<Degree> degrees;

public long getId() {
  return id;
}

public void setId(long id) {
  this.id = id;
}

public String getName() {
  return name;
}

public void setName(String name) {
  this.name = name;
}

public List<Degree> getDegrees() {
  return degrees;
}

public void setDegrees(List<Degree> degrees) {
  this.degrees = degrees;
}

@Override
public String toString() {
  return "Employee "
      + "\n\tId: " + this.id
      + "\n\tName: " + this.name
      + "\n\tDegrees: " + this.degrees;
}
}
```

When we create `SessionFactory` with the `hbm2dll=create|update` option, hibernate will create the `employee`, `degree` and `employee_degree` tables for us; otherwise, you can use the following table script:

degree	employee	employee_degree
id (PK)	id (PK)	employee_id (FK)
degreename	name	degrees_id (FK)
passingyear		

Creating tables

Use the following script to create tables if you are not using `hbm2dll=create|update`. This script is for the tables that are generated by hibernate.

Use the following code to create the `degree` table:

```
CREATE TABLE `degree` (
  `id` bigint(20) NOT NULL AUTO_INCREMENT,
  `degreename` varchar(255) DEFAULT NULL,
  `passingyear` int(11) DEFAULT NULL,
  PRIMARY KEY (`id`)
);
```

Use the following code to create the `employee` table:

```
CREATE TABLE `employee` (
  `id` bigint(20) NOT NULL AUTO_INCREMENT,
  `name` varchar(255) DEFAULT NULL,
  PRIMARY KEY (`id`)
);
```

Use the following code to create the `employee_degree` table:

```
CREATE TABLE `employee_degree` (
  `employee_id` bigint(20) NOT NULL,
  `degrees_id` bigint(20) NOT NULL,
  UNIQUE KEY `degrees_id` (`degrees_id`),
  KEY `FK9CF457D5DB631AF` (`degrees_id`),
  KEY `FK9CF457D699100AA` (`employee_id`),
  CONSTRAINT `FK9CF457D699100AA` FOREIGN KEY (`employee_id`)
REFERENCES `employee` (`id`),
  CONSTRAINT `FK9CF457D5DB631AF` FOREIGN KEY (`degrees_id`)
REFERENCES `degree` (`id`)
);
```

Here, we used `@OneToMany(cascade={CascadeType.ALL})` to map `degree` with `employee`.

Refer to the following code that shows how to insert/display records.

Inserting a record

Here, we insert one `employee` record with the two degrees associated with this employee.

Code

Use the following code to insert an `employee` record with degrees:

```
Employee employee = new Employee();
employee.setName("yogesh");
```

```
List<Degree> degrees = new ArrayList<Degree>();
degrees.add(new Degree("B.E.", 2008));
degrees.add(new Degree("M.S.", 2011));

employee.setDegrees(degrees);

session.getTransaction().begin();
session.save(employee);
session.getTransaction().commit();
```

Output

```
Hibernate: insert into employee (name) values (?)
Hibernate: insert into degree (degreename, passingyear) values (?,
?)
Hibernate: insert into degree (degreename, passingyear) values (?,
?)
Hibernate: insert into employee_degree (employee_id, degrees_id)
values (?, ?)
Hibernate: insert into employee_degree (employee_id, degrees_id)
values (?, ?)
```

Here, from the SQL statements, we understand that the first SQL statement inserts one record in to the employee table, the next two statements create two records in the degree table, and the last two statements create the mapping records in the employee_degree table using the inserted values of both the employee and degree tables.

Retrieving a record

Here, we will fetch the record of Employee#1 from the database. Use the following code to do so:

Code

```
Employee employee = (Employee) session.get(Employee.class, 1l);
System.out.println(employee.toString());
```

Output

```
Hibernate: select employee0_.id as id0_0_, employee0_.name as
name0_0_ from employee employee0_ where employee0_.id=?
Hibernate: select degrees0_.employee_id as employee1_0_1_,
degrees0_.degrees_id as degrees2_1_, degree1_.id as id1_0_,
degree1_.degreename as degreename1_0_, degree1_.passingyear as
passingy3_1_0_ from employee_degree degrees0_ inner join degree
degree1_ on degrees0_.degrees_id=degree1_.id where degrees0_.employee_
id=?
Employee
   Id: 1
```

```
   Name: yogesh
   Degrees: [

Degree
   Id: 1
   Name: B.E.
   Passing year: 2008,

Degree
   Id: 2
   Name: M.S.
   Passing year: 2011]
```

Persisting Set

`Set` provides an unordered data structure, and duplicate elements are not allowed. Some classes implemented by the `Set` interface are `java.util.HashSet`, `java.util.LinkedHashSet`, and so on. For this recipe, we will use the `java.util.HashSet` class, which implements the `java.util.Set` interface. The only difference between `List` and `Set` is that `Set` doesn't allow duplicate values. For example, in our previous example, we added the e-mail address with `emailaddress3@provider3.com` twice, and hibernate will allow us to do this. But in case of `Set`, you cannot add a duplicate value. Let's take a look at how to achieve this.

Getting ready

Now, we need the class to persist `Set` in hibernate. Use the next code snippet to create the `Employee` class.

Creating a class

Use the following code to create the classes:

Source file: `Employee.java`

```
@Entity
@Table(name = "employee")
public class Employee {

   @Id
   @GeneratedValue
   @Column(name = "id")
   private long id;
```

```
    @Column(name = "name")
    private String name;

    @ElementCollection
    @CollectionTable(name = "email")
    private Set<String> emails;

    public long getId() {
      return id;
    }

    public void setId(long id) {
      this.id = id;
    }

    public String getName() {
      return name;
    }

    public void setName(String name) {
      this.name = name;
    }

    public Set<String> getEmails() {
      return emails;
    }

    public void setEmails(Set<String> emails) {
      this.emails = emails;
    }

    @Override
    public String toString() {
      return "Employee"
          + "\n\tId: " + this.id
          + "\n\tName: " + this.name
          + "\n\tEmails: " + this.emails;
    }

}
```

How to do it...

Here, we will discuss how to persist `Set` and also the manipulation operations with `Set`, such as inserting, retrieving, deleting, and updating.

Inserting a record

Here, we create the employee record with some e-mail addresses of the employee.

From the code's point of view, there are fewer changes as compared to `List`. This is because this relationship is not directly known to the database but virtually created by hibernate. Use the following code to do so:

Code

```
    SessionFactory sessionFactory =
HibernateUtil.getSessionFactory();
    Session session = sessionFactory.openSession();

    Employee employee = new Employee();
    employee.setName("yogesh");

    Set<String> emails = new HashSet<String>();
    emails.add("emailaddress1@provider1.com");
    emails.add("emailaddress2@provider2.com");
    emails.add("emailaddress3@provider3.com");
    employee.setEmails(emails);

    session.getTransaction().begin();
    session.save(employee);
    session.getTransaction().commit();
```

Output

```
    Hibernate: insert into employee (name) values (?)
    Hibernate: insert into email (Employee_id, emails) values (?, ?)
    Hibernate: insert into email (Employee_id, emails) values (?, ?)
    Hibernate: insert into email (Employee_id, emails) values (?, ?)
```

When the code is executed, it inserts one record into the `employee` table and three records into the `email` table, and it also sets a primary key value for the `employee` record in each record of the `email` table as a reference.

Retrieving a record

Here, we know that our record is inserted with `id` 1. So, we will try to get only this record and understand how `Set` works in our case:

Code

```
Employee employee = (Employee) session.get(Employee.class, 1l);
System.out.println(employee.toString());
```

Output

```
Hibernate: select employee0_.id as id0_0_, employee0_.name as
name0_0_ from employee employee0_ where employee0_.id=?
Hibernate: select emails0_.Employee_id as Employee1_0_0_,
emails0_.emails as emails0_ from email emails0_ where
emails0_.Employee_id=?
Employee
  Id: 1
  Name: yogesh
  Emails: [emailaddress1@provider1.com,
emailaddress2@provider2.com,    emailaddress3@provider3.com]
```

Updating a record

Here, we will try to add one more e-mail address to `Employee#1`:

Code

```
Employee employee = (Employee) session.get(Employee.class, 1l);
Set<String> emails = employee.getEmails();
emails.add("emailaddress3@provider3.com");
session.getTransaction().begin();
session.saveOrUpdate(employee);
session.getTransaction().commit();
System.out.println(employee.toString());
```

Output

```
Hibernate: select employee0_.id as id0_0_, employee0_.name as
name0_0_ from employee employee0_ where employee0_.id=?
Hibernate: select emails0_.Employee_id as Employee1_0_0_,
emails0_.emails as emails0_ from email emails0_ where
emails0_.Employee_id=?
Employee
  Id: 1
  Name: yogesh
  Emails: [emailaddress2@provider2.com,
emailaddress1@provider1.com  emailaddress3@provider3.com]
```

Here, we can see that we tried to add the e-mail address, `emailaddress3@provider3.com`, which is already in `List`; therefore, hibernate doesn't execute an update query to the database. This is because `Set` doesn't allow duplicate values.

Deleting a record

Here again, we will try to delete the `Employee#1` object. Use the following code to do so:

Code

```
Employee employee = new Employee();
employee.setId(1);
session.getTransaction().begin();
session.delete(employee);
session.getTransaction().commit();
```

Output

```
Hibernate: delete from email where Employee_id=?
Hibernate: delete from employee where id=?
```

While deleting the object, hibernate will delete the child records (here, e-mail addresses) as well. This works in the same way as `List`.

How it works...

The implementation of `Set` is the same as that of `List`, because this relationship is handled by hibernate only and is not directly known by the database. Also, hibernate creates the same table structure as `List`, as shown in table below:

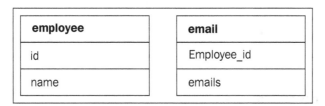

employee	email
id	Employee_id
name	emails

Persisting Map

`Map` is used when we want to persist a collection of key/value pairs where the key is always unique. Some common implementations of `java.util.Map` are `java.util.HashMap`, `java.util.LinkedHashMap`, and so on. For this recipe, we will use `java.util.HashMap`.

Getting ready

Now, let's assume that we have a scenario where we are going to implement `Map<String, String>`; here, the `String` key is the e-mail address label, and the value `String` is the e-mail address. For example, we will try to construct a data structure similar to `<"Personal e-mail", "emailaddress2@provider2.com">, <"Business e-mail", "emailaddress1@provider1.com">`. This means that we will create an alias of the actual e-mail address so that we can easily get the e-mail address using the alias and can document it in a more readable form. This type of implementation depends on the custom requirement; here, we can easily get a business e-mail using the `Business email` key.

Use the following code to create the required tables and classes.

Creating tables

Use the following script to create the tables if you are not using `hbm2dll=create|update`. This script is for the tables that are generated by hibernate:

Use the following code to create the `email` table:

```
CREATE TABLE `email` (
  `Employee_id` BIGINT(20) NOT NULL,
  `emails` VARCHAR(255) DEFAULT NULL,
  `emails_KEY` VARCHAR(255) NOT NULL DEFAULT '',
  PRIMARY KEY (`Employee_id`,`emails_KEY`),
  KEY `FK5C24B9C38F47B40` (`Employee_id`),
  CONSTRAINT `FK5C24B9C38F47B40` FOREIGN KEY (`Employee_id`)
REFERENCES `employee` (`id`)
);
```

Use the following code to create the `employee` table:

```
CREATE TABLE `employee` (
  `id` BIGINT(20) NOT NULL AUTO_INCREMENT,
  `name` VARCHAR(255) DEFAULT NULL,
  PRIMARY KEY (`id`)
);
```

Creating a class

Source file: `Employee.java`

```
@Entity
@Table(name = "employee")
public class Employee {

    @Id
```

```
@GeneratedValue
@Column(name = "id")
private long id;

@Column(name = "name")
private String name;

@ElementCollection
@CollectionTable(name = "email")
private Map<String, String> emails;

public long getId() {
  return id;
}

public void setId(long id) {
  this.id = id;
}

public String getName() {
  return name;
}

public void setName(String name) {
  this.name = name;
}

public Map<String, String> getEmails() {
  return emails;
}

public void setEmails(Map<String, String> emails) {
  this.emails = emails;
}

@Override
public String toString() {
  return "Employee"
      + "\n\tId: " + this.id
      + "\n\tName: " + this.name
      + "\n\tEmails: " + this.emails;
}
}
```

How to do it...

Here, we will consider how to work with `Map` and its manipulation operations, such as inserting, retrieving, deleting, and updating.

Inserting a record

Here, we will create one `employee` record with two e-mail addresses:

Code

```
Employee employee = new Employee();
employee.setName("yogesh");

Map<String, String> emails = new HashMap<String, String>();
emails.put("Business email", "emailaddress1@provider1.com");
emails.put("Personal email", "emailaddress2@provider2.com");
employee.setEmails(emails);

session.getTransaction().begin();
session.save(employee);
session.getTransaction().commit();
```

Output

```
Hibernate: insert into employee (name) values (?)
Hibernate: insert into email (Employee_id, emails_KEY, emails)
values (?,?,?)
Hibernate: insert into email (Employee_id, emails_KEY, emails)
values (?,?,?)
```

When the code is executed, it inserts one record into the `employee` table and two records into the `email` table and also sets a primary key value for the `employee` record in each record of the `email` table as a reference.

Retrieving a record

Here, we know that our record is inserted with `id` 1. So, we will try to get only that record and understand how `Map` works in our case.

Code

```
Employee employee = (Employee) session.get(Employee.class, 1l);
System.out.println(employee.toString());
System.out.println("Business email: " +
employee.getEmails().get("Business email"));
```

```
Hibernate: select employee0_.id as id0_0_, employee0_.name as
name0_0_ from employee employee0_ where employee0_.id=?
Hibernate: select emails0_.Employee_id as Employee1_0_0_,
emails0_.emails as emails0_, emails0_.emails_KEY as emails3_0_
from email emails0_ where emails0_.Employee_id=?
Employee
  Id: 1
  Name: yogesh
  Emails: {Personal email=emailaddress2@provider2.com, Business
email=emailaddress1@provider1.com}
  Business email: emailaddress1@provider1.com
```

Here, we can easily get a business e-mail address using the `Business email` key from the map of e-mail addresses. This is just a simple scenario created to demonstrate how to persist `Map` in hibernate.

Updating a record

Here, we will try to add one more e-mail address to `Employee#1`:

Code

```
Employee employee = (Employee) session.get(Employee.class, 1l);
Map<String, String> emails = employee.getEmails();
emails.put("Personal email 1", "emailaddress3@provider3.com");
session.getTransaction().begin();
session.saveOrUpdate(employee);
session.getTransaction().commit();
System.out.println(employee.toString());
```

Output

```
Hibernate: select employee0_.id as id0_0_, employee0_.name as
name0_0_ from employee employee0_ where employee0_.id=?
Hibernate: select emails0_.Employee_id as Employee1_0_0_,
emails0_.emails as emails0_, emails0_.emails_KEY as emails3_0_
from email emails0_ where emails0_.Employee_id=?
Hibernate: insert into email (Employee_id, emails_KEY, emails)
values (?, ?, ?)
Employee
  Id: 2
  Name: yogesh
  Emails: {Personal email 1= emailaddress3@provider3.com, Personal
email=emailaddress2@provider2.com, Business
email=emailaddress1@provider1.com}
```

Here, we added a new e-mail address with the `Personal email 1` key and the value is `emailaddress3@provider3.com`.

Deleting a record

Here again, we will try to delete the records of `Employee#1` using the following code:

Code

```
Employee employee = new Employee();
employee.setId(1);
session.getTransaction().begin();
session.delete(employee);
session.getTransaction().commit();
```

Output

```
Hibernate: delete from email where Employee_id=?
Hibernate: delete from employee where id=?
```

While deleting the object, hibernate will delete the child records (here, e-mail addresses) as well.

How it works...

Here again, we need to understand the table structures created by hibernate:

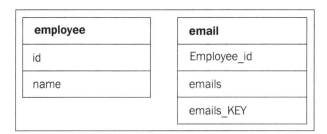

This is the same as in all the other examples in this chapter. Hibernate creates a composite primary key in the `email` table using two fields: `employee_id` and `emails_KEY`.

Persisting Array

Working with `Array` is similar to that with `List`, but in `List`, it is not compulsory to add `@IndexColumn`. However, `Array` requires an indexed column to maintain the column order.

Getting ready

Create the required class using the following code to persist `Array`:

Source file: `Employee.java`

```
@Entity
@Table(name = "employee")
public class Employee {

  @Id
  @GeneratedValue
  @Column (name = "id")
  private long id;

  @Column (name = "name")
  private String name;

  @ElementCollection
  @IndexColumn(name="email_index")
  @CollectionTable(name = "email")
  private String[] emails;

  public long getId() {
    return id;
  }

  public void setId(long id) {
    this.id = id;
  }

  public String getName() {
    return name;
  }

  public void setName(String name) {
    this.name = name;
  }

  public String[] getEmails() {
    return emails;
  }

  public void setEmails(String[] emails) {
```

```
    this.emails = emails;
  }


  @Override
  public String toString() {
    return "Employee"
    + "\n\tId: " + this.id + "\n\tName: " + this.name
        + "\n\tEmails: " + Arrays.toString(this.emails);
  }
}
```

How to do it...

We will take a look at how to insert and retrieve the data from hibernate using `Array`.

Inserting a record

Here, we create one `employee` record with `Array` of e-mail addresses. Use the following code to do so:

Code

```
Employee employee = new Employee();
employee.setName("vishal");
employee.setEmails (new String []{"emailaddress1@provider1.com",
"emailaddress2@provider2.com", "emailaddress3@provider3.com",
"emailaddress4@provider4.com"});

session.getTransaction().begin();
session.save(employee);
session.getTransaction().commit();
```

Output

```
Hibernate: insert into employee (name) values (?)
Hibernate: insert into email (Employee_id, email_index, emails)
values (?,?,?)
Hibernate: insert into email (Employee_id, email_index, emails)
values (?,?,?)
Hibernate: insert into email (Employee_id, email_index, emails)
values (?,?,?)
Hibernate: insert into email (Employee_id, email_index, emails)
values (?,?,?)
```

Retrieving a record

Use the following code to retrieve records for `Employee#1`:

Code

```
Employee employee = (Employee) session.get(Employee.class, 11);
System.out.println(employee.toString());
```

Output

```
Hibernate: select employee0_.id as id0_0_, employee0_.name as
name0_0_ from employee employee0_ where employee0_.id=?
Hibernate: select emails0_.Employee_id as Employee1_0_0_,
emails0_.emails as emails0_, emails0_.email_index as email3_0_
from email emails0_ where emails0_.Employee_id=?
Employee
  Id: 1
  Name: vishal
  Emails: [emailaddress1@provider1.com,
emailaddress2@provider2.com,  emailaddress3@provider3.com,
emailaddress4@provider4.com]
```

5
Working with Associations

In this chapter, we will cover the following recipes:

- ▸ One-to-one mapping using a foreign key association
- ▸ One-to-one mapping using a common join table
- ▸ One-to-one mapping using a common primary key
- ▸ One-to-many mapping or many-to-one mapping
- ▸ Many-to-many mapping

Introduction

An association represents the relationship between tables. There are two main types of associations: unidirectional and bidirectional. We will take a look at how to use associations with an example.

There are four main well-known types of relationships:

- ▸ One-to-one
- ▸ One-to-many
- ▸ Many-to-one
- ▸ Many-to-many

There are multiple ways to achieve these relationships.

One-to-one mapping using foreign key association

In a one-to-one relationship, each row in the first table is linked to exactly one row in another table. If this relationship is applied, we can say that both the tables have an exactly equal number of rows any time.

We will take a look at the unidirectional and bidirectional ways to show a one-to-one relationship between the tables.

Getting ready

Here, we will consider the `Person` and `PersonDetail` classes to show a demo. So, let's first create the classes and tables for both.

Creating the tables

Use the following script to create the tables if you are not using `hbm2dll=create|update`:

Use the following script to create the `passport_detail` table:

```
CREATE TABLE `passport_detail` (
  `id` bigint(20) NOT NULL AUTO_INCREMENT,
  `passportno` varchar(255) DEFAULT NULL,
  PRIMARY KEY (`id`)
);
```

Use the following script to create the `person` table:

```
CREATE TABLE `person` (
  `id` bigint(20) NOT NULL AUTO_INCREMENT,
  `name` varchar(255) DEFAULT NULL,
  `passport_detail_id` bigint(20) DEFAULT NULL,
  PRIMARY KEY (`id`),
  KEY `FK_PERSON_ID` (`passport_detail_id`),
  CONSTRAINT `FK_PERSON_ID` FOREIGN KEY (`passport_detail_id`)
REFERENCES `passport_detail` (`id`)
);
```

Creating the classes

Use the following code to create the classes:

Source file: `PassportDetail.java`

```java
@Entity
@Table(name = "passport_detail")
public class PassportDetail {

  @Id
  @GeneratedValue
  @Column(name = "id")
  private long id;

  @Column(name = "passportno")
  private String passportNo;

  public long getId() {
    return id;
  }

  public void setId(long id) {
    this.id = id;
  }

  public String getPassportNo() {
    return passportNo;
  }

  public void setPassportNo(String passportNo) {
    this.passportNo = passportNo;
  }

}
```

Source file: `Person.java`

```java
@Entity
@Table(name = "person")
public class Person {

  @Id
  @GeneratedValue
  @Column(name = "id")
  private long id;

  @Column(name = "name")
```

```
    private String name;

    @OneToOne(cascade = CascadeType.ALL)
    @JoinColumn(name = "passport_detail_id")
    private PassportDetail passportDetail;

    public long getId() {
      return id;
    }

    public void setId(long id) {
      this.id = id;
    }

    public String getName() {
      return name;
    }

    public void setName(String name) {
      this.name = name;
    }

    public PassportDetail getPassportDetail() {
      return passportDetail;
    }
}

    public void setPassportDetail(PassportDetail passportDetail) {
      this.passportDetail = passportDetail;
    }

}
```

How to do it...

In this section, we will take a look at how to insert a record step by step.

Inserting a record

Using the following code, we will insert a `Person` object with a `PassportDetail` one:

Code

```
    PassportDetail detail = new PassportDetail();
    detail.setPassportNo("G51546645");

    Person person = new Person();
    person.setName("Vishal");
```

```
person.setPassportDetail(detail);

Transaction transaction = session.getTransaction();
transaction.begin();

session.save(person);
transaction.commit();
```

Output

```
Hibernate: insert into passport_detail (passportno) values (?)
Hibernate: insert into person (name, passport_detail_id) values
(?,?)
```

Here, we created `PassportDetail` and `Person` objects and saved both to the database.

How it works...

Here, the one-to-one relationship is not directly known to the database, but it is created for simplicity purposes and is useful to define a user-specific scenario. This means that each `Person` has one and only one `PassportDetail` object, and `PassportDetail` does not exist without `Person`.

As we used the `@OneToOne` annotation in the preceding code, hibernate will consider that we want to have a one-to-one relationship between both the tables.

Let's take a look at an option used in the preceding code in detail:

`cascade=CascadeType.ALL:`

This option in the `@OneToOne` annotation shows that hibernate uses cascading for all database operations. Here, we save a `Person` record, but before saving a `Person` object, it saves a `PassportDetail` object because `PassportDetail` is referred to by the `Person` object. If the `PassportDetail` object is not persisted at the time of saving the `Person` object, and the appropriate `CascadeType` option is not used, it throws an error similar to `"Exception in thread "main" org.hibernate.TransientObjectException: object references an unsaved transient instance - save the transient instance before flushing: "PassportDetail"`.

The `@JoinColumn` annotation is used to define the relationship between tables—in our case, between the `person` table and a column created with the name `"passport_detail_id"`— and it refers to the primary key of the `" "passport_detail "` table, which is `"id"`.

In other words, it creates a foreign key reference.

There's more...

Here, we will take a look at the bidirectional way to achieve the relationship.

The logic behind this technique is that each row in the parent table knows its child record identity, and each row from child table knows its parent record identity. For example, in our case, `Person` knows its `PassportDetail` record, and `PassportDetail` knows its `Person` record; so, we can get the detail for both using any one table.

Here, we will use the same tables/classes structure as the one in the previous section with minor changes.

Creating the tables

Use the following script to create the tables if you are not using `hbm2dll=create|update`:

Use the following script to create the `passport_detail` table:

```
CREATE TABLE `passport_detail` (
  `id` bigint(20) NOT NULL AUTO_INCREMENT,
  `passportno` varchar(255) DEFAULT NULL,
  PRIMARY KEY (`id`)
);
```

Use the following script to create the `passport_detail` table:

```
CREATE TABLE `person` (
  `id` bigint(20) NOT NULL AUTO_INCREMENT,
  `name` varchar(255) DEFAULT NULL,
  `passport_detail_id` bigint(20) DEFAULT NULL,
  PRIMARY KEY (`id`),
  KEY `FK_PERSON_ID` (`passport_detail_id`),
  CONSTRAINT `FK_PERSON_ID` FOREIGN KEY (`passport_detail_id`)
REFERENCES `passport_detail` (`id`)
);
```

Creating the classes

Use the following code to create the classes:

Source file: `Person.java`

```
@Entity
@Table(name = "person")
public class Person {

  @Id
  @GeneratedValue
```

```java
@Column(name = "id")
private long id;

@Column(name = "name")
private String name;

@OneToOne(cascade = CascadeType.ALL)
@JoinColumn(name = "passport_detail_id")
private PassportDetail passportDetail;

public long getId() {
  return id;
}

public void setId(long id) {
  this.id = id;
}

public String getName() {
  return name;
}

public void setName(String name) {
  this.name = name;
}

public PassportDetail getPassportDetail() {
  return passportDetail;
}

public void setPassportDetail(PassportDetail passportDetail) {
  this.passportDetail = passportDetail;
}

@Override
public String toString() {
  return "Person"

    +"\n Id: " + this.id
    +"\n Name: " + this.name
    +"\n Passport Detail "
    + "\n\t Id: " + this.passportDetail.getId()
    + "\n\t PassportNo: " + this.passportDetail.getPassportNo();

  }

}
```

Source file: `PersonDetail.java`

```
@Entity
@Table(name = "passport_detail")
public class PassportDetail {

  @Id
  @GeneratedValue
  @Column(name = "id")
  private long id;

  @Column(name = "passportno")
  private String passportNo;

  @OneToOne(mappedBy = "passportDetail", cascade =
CascadeType.ALL)
  private Person person;

  public long getId() {
    return id;
  }

  public void setId(long id) {
    this.id = id;
  }

  public String getPassportNo() {
    return passportNo;
  }

  public void setPassportNo(String passportNo) {
    this.passportNo = passportNo;
  }

  public Person getPerson() {
    return person;
  }

  public void setPerson(Person person) {
    this.person = person;
  }

  @Override
  public String toString() {
    return "Passport Detail"
```

```
+"\n Id: " + this.id
+"\n Name: " + this.getPassportNo()
+"\n Person "
+ "\n\t Id: " + this.person.getId()
+ "\n\t PassportNo: " + this.person.getName();


}
```

Inserting a record

Here, we will insert a `Person` object with a `PassportDetail`:

Code

```
PassportDetail detail = new PassportDetail();
detail.setPassportNo("G54624512");

Person person = new Person();
person.setName("Yogesh");
person.setPassportDetail(detail);

Transaction transaction = session.getTransaction();
transaction.begin();

session.save(person);
transaction.commit();
```

Output

```
Hibernate: insert into passport_detail (passportno) values (?)
Hibernate: insert into person (name, passport_detail_id) values
(?,?)
```

Retrieving a record using the parent record

Now, we will try to get a `PassportDetail` (child) record using a `Person` (parent) record.
Execute the following code:

Code

```
Criteria criteria = session.createCriteria(Person.class);
Person person = (Person) criteria.uniqueResult();
System.out.println(person.toString());
```

Output

```
Hibernate: select this_.id as id1_1_1_, this_.name as name2_1_1_,
this_.passport_detail_id as passport3_1_1_, passportde2_.id as
id1_0_0_, passportde2_.passportno as passport2_0_0_ from person
this_ left outer join passport_detail passportde2_ on
this_.passport_detail_id=passportde2_.id
```

```
Hibernate: select person0_.id as id1_1_1_, person0_.name as
name2_1_1_, person0_.passport_detail_id as passport3_1_1_,
passportde1_.id as id1_0_0_, passportde1_.passportno as
passport2_0_0_ from person person0_ left outer join
passport_detail passportde1_ on
person0_.passport_detail_id=passportde1_.id where
person0_.passport_detail_id=?


Person
  Id: 1
  Name: Yogesh
  Passport Detail
    Id: 1
    PassportNo: G54624512
```

Retrieving a record using the child record

Now, we will do the inverse of the preceding example and try to get a `Person` (parent) record using a `PassportDetail` (child) record:

Code

```
Criteria criteria =
session.createCriteria(PassportDetail.class);
PassportDetail passportDetail = (PassportDetail)
criteria.uniqueResult();
System.out.println(passportDetail.toString());
```

Output

```
Hibernate: select this_.id as id1_0_1_, this_.passportno as
passport2_0_1_, person2_.id as id1_1_0_, person2_.name as
name2_1_0_, person2_.passport_detail_id as passport3_1_0_ from
passport_detail this_ left outer join person person2_ on
this_.id=person2_.passport_detail_id


Passport Detail
 Id: 1
 PassportNoName: G54624512
 Person
   Id: 1
   PassportNoName: Yogesh
```

One-to-one mapping using a common join table

In this method, we will use a third table that contains the relationship between the employee and detail tables. In other words, the third table will hold a primary key value of both tables to represent a relationship between them.

Getting ready

Use the following script to create the tables and classes. Here, we use `Employee` and `EmployeeDetail` to show a one-to-one mapping using a common join table:

Creating the tables

Use the following script to create the tables if you are not using `hbm2dll=create|update`:

Use the following script to create the `detail` table:

```
CREATE TABLE `detail` (
  `detail_id` bigint(20) NOT NULL AUTO_INCREMENT,
  `city` varchar(255) DEFAULT NULL,
  PRIMARY KEY (`detail_id`)
);
```

Use the following script to create the `employee` table:

```
CREATE TABLE `employee` (
  `employee_id` BIGINT(20) NOT NULL AUTO_INCREMENT,
  `name` VARCHAR(255) DEFAULT NULL,
  PRIMARY KEY (`employee_id`)
);
```

Use the following script to create the `employee_detail` table:

```
CREATE TABLE `employee_detail` (
  `detail_id` BIGINT(20) DEFAULT NULL,
  `employee_id` BIGINT(20) NOT NULL,
  PRIMARY KEY (`employee_id`),
  KEY `FK_DETAIL_ID` (`detail_id`),
  KEY `FK_EMPLOYEE_ID` (`employee_id`),
  CONSTRAINT `FK_EMPLOYEE_ID`
    FOREIGN KEY (`employee_id`)
    REFERENCES `employee` (`employee_id`),
  CONSTRAINT `FK_DETAIL_ID`
    FOREIGN KEY (`detail_id`)
    REFERENCES `detail` (`detail_id`)
);
```

Creating the classes

Use the following code to create the classes:

Source file: `Employee.java`

```java
@Entity
@Table(name = "employee")
public class Employee {

  @Id
  @GeneratedValue
  @Column(name = "employee_id")
  private long id;

  @Column(name = "name")
  private String name;

  @OneToOne(cascade = CascadeType.ALL)
  @JoinTable(
    name="employee_detail"
    , joinColumns=@JoinColumn(name="employee_id")
    , inverseJoinColumns=@JoinColumn(name="detail_id")
  )
  private Detail employeeDetail;

  public long getId() {
    return id;
  }

  public void setId(long id) {
    this.id = id;
  }

  public String getName() {
    return name;
  }

  public void setName(String name) {
    this.name = name;
  }

  public Detail getEmployeeDetail() {
    return employeeDetail;
  }

  public void setEmployeeDetail(Detail employeeDetail) {
    this.employeeDetail = employeeDetail;
```

```
    }

    @Override
    public String toString() {
      return "Employee"
        +"\n Id: " + this.id
        +"\n Name: " + this.name
        +"\n Employee Detail "
        + "\n\t Id: " + this.employeeDetail.getId()
        + "\n\t City: " +
          this.employeeDetail.getCity();

    }

  }
```

Source file: `Detail.java`

```
@Entity
@Table(name = "detail")
public class Detail {

  @Id
  @GeneratedValue
  @Column(name = "detail_id")
  private long id;

  @Column(name = "city")
  private String city;

  @OneToOne(cascade = CascadeType.ALL)
  @JoinTable(
    name="employee_detail"
    , joinColumns=@JoinColumn(name="detail_id")
    , inverseJoinColumns=@JoinColumn(name="employee_id")
  )
  private Employee employee;

  public Employee getEmployee() {
    return employee;
  }

  public void setEmployee(Employee employee) {
    this.employee = employee;
  }
```

```
   public String getCity() {
     return city;
   }

   public void setCity(String city) {
     this.city = city;
   }

   public long getId() {
     return id;
   }

   public void setId(long id) {
     this.id = id;
   }

   @Override
   public String toString() {
     return "Employee Detail"
       +"\n Id: " + this.id
       +"\n City: " + this.city
       +"\n Employee "
       + "\n\t Id: " + this.employee.getId()
       + "\n\t Name: " + this.employee.getName();


   }

}
```

How to do it...

In this section, we will take a look at how to insert a record step by step.

Inserting a record

Using the following code, we will insert an Employee record with a Detail object:

Code

```
Detail detail = new Detail();
detail.setCity("AHM");

Employee employee = new Employee();
employee.setName("vishal");
employee.setEmployeeDetail(detail);
```

```
Transaction transaction = session.getTransaction();
transaction.begin();

session.save(employee);
transaction.commit();
```

Output

```
Hibernate: insert into detail (city) values (?)
Hibernate: insert into employee (name) values (?)
Hibernate: insert into employee_detail (detail_id, employee_id)
values (?,?)
```

Hibernate saves one record in the `detail` table and one in the `employee` table and then inserts a record in to the third table, `employee_detail`, using the primary key column value of the `detail` and `employee` tables.

How it works...

From the output, it's clear how this method works. The code is the same as in the other methods of configuring a one-to-one relationship, but here, hibernate reacts differently. Here, the first two statements of output insert the records in to the `detail` and `employee` tables respectively, and the third statement inserts the mapping record in to the third table, `employee_detail`, using the primary key column value of both the tables.

Let's take a look at an option used in the previous code in detail:

- ▶ `@JoinTable`: This annotation, written on the `Employee` class, contains the `name="employee_detail"` attribute and shows that a new intermediate table is created with the name `"employee_detail"`
- ▶ `joinColumns=@JoinColumn(name="employee_id")`: This shows that a reference column is created in `employee_detail` with the name `"employee_id"`, which is the primary key of the `employee` table
- ▶ `inverseJoinColumns=@JoinColumn(name="detail_id")`: This shows that a reference column is created in the `employee_detail` table with the name `"detail_id"`, which is the primary key of the detail table

Ultimately, the third table, `employee_detail`, is created with two columns: one is `"employee_id"` and the other is `"detail_id"`.

One-to-one mapping using a common primary key

In this method, we will create a relationship in such a way that both tables contain the same primary key value for the related record. So, we can say that here we used unidirectional as well as bidirectional relationships, because we can get either record through another record using its primary key. For example, if `Person` is inserted with id 1, you should get the `PassportDetail` record inserted with id 1 as well.

Getting ready

Here, we will create `Person` and `PassportDetail` classes to work this demo.

Creating the tables

Use the following script to create the tables if you are not using hbm2dll=create|update:

Use the following script to create the `passport_detail` table:

```
CREATE TABLE `passport_detail` (
  `id` bigint(20) NOT NULL AUTO_INCREMENT,
  `passportno` varchar(255) DEFAULT NULL,
  PRIMARY KEY (`id`)
);
```

Use the following script to create the `person` table:

```
CREATE TABLE `person` (
  `id` bigint(20) NOT NULL AUTO_INCREMENT,
  `name` varchar(255) DEFAULT NULL,
  PRIMARY KEY (`id`),
  KEY `FK_PASSPORT_DETAIL_ID` (`id`),
  CONSTRAINT `FK_PASSPORT_DETAIL_ID`
    FOREIGN KEY (`id`)
    REFERENCES `passport_detail` (`id`)
);
```

Creating the classes

Here, we will use `Person` and `PassportDetail` classes:

Source file: `Person.java`

```
@Entity
@Table(name = "person")
public class Person {
```

```java
    @Id
    @GeneratedValue
    @Column(name = "id")
    private long id;

    @Column(name = "name")
    private String name;

    @OneToOne(cascade = CascadeType.ALL)
    @PrimaryKeyJoinColumn
    private PassportDetail passportDetail;

    public long getId() {
      return id;
    }

    public void setId(long id) {
      this.id = id;
    }

    public String getName() {
      return name;
    }

    public void setName(String name) {
      this.name = name;
    }

    public PassportDetail getPassportDetail() {
      return passportDetail;
    }

    public void setPassportDetail(PassportDetail passportDetail) {
      this.passportDetail = passportDetail;
    }

  }
```

Source file: `PassportDetail.java`

```java
    @Entity
    @Table(name = "passport_detail")
    public class PassportDetail {
```

```
   @Id
   @GeneratedValue
   @Column(name = "id")
   private long id;

   @Column(name = "passportno")
   private String passportNo;

   @OneToOne(
     mappedBy = "passportDetail"
     , cascade =   CascadeType.ALL
   )
   private Person person;

   public long getId() {
     return id;
   }

   public void setId(long id) {
     this.id = id;
   }

   public String getPassportNo() {
     return passportNo;
   }

   public void setPassportNo(String passportNo) {
     this.passportNo = passportNo;
   }

   public Person getPerson() {
     return person;
   }

   public void setPerson(Person person) {
     this.person = person;
   }

}
```

How to do it...

In this section, we will take a look at how to insert a record step by step.

Inserting a record

Use the following code to insert a record in to the database. Here, we will insert a `Person` with a `PassportDetail` object:

Code

```
PassportDetail detail = new PassportDetail();
detail.setPassportNo("G44244781");

Person person = new Person();
person.setId(1);
person.setName("Virendra");
person.setPassportDetail(detail);

Transaction transaction = session.getTransaction();
transaction.begin();
session.save(person);
transaction.commit();
```

Output

```
Hibernate: insert into passport_detail (passportno) values (?)
Hibernate: insert into person (name) values (?)
```

How it works...

Let's start with the changes in the `PassportDetail` class.

The first change is in `@OneToOne(cascade = CascadeType.ALL)`.

Here, we used `@OneToOne` with the `CascadeType.ALL` option, which informs hibernate to create a one-to-one relationship and apply cascading for all operations.

The changes in the `Person` class are as follows:

- `@PrimaryKeyJoinColumn`
- `private PassportDetail passportDetail;`

The `@PrimaryKeyJoinColumn` annotation is used with the `PassportDetail` class, which creates a reference between the primary key of the `Person` class and the primary key of the `PassportDetail` class.

One-to-many mapping or many-to-one mapping

Here, we will create a different scenario for a better understanding of the relationship. We will take a look at the use of both one-to-many and many-to-one relationships in a single example.

Now, we will create a relationship between actor and movie tables, where one actor is associated with one movie, but one movie can be associated with multiple actors.

Getting ready

We will create the classes and tables for `Movie` and `Actor`.

Creating the tables

Use the following script to create the tables if you are not using `hbm2dll=create|update`:

Use the following script to create the `movie` table:

```
CREATE TABLE `movie` (
  `id` bigint(20) NOT NULL AUTO_INCREMENT,
  `name` varchar(255) DEFAULT NULL,
  PRIMARY KEY (`id`)
)
```

Use the following script to create the `actor` table:

```
CREATE TABLE `actor` (
  `id` bigint(20) NOT NULL AUTO_INCREMENT,
  `actorname` varchar(255) DEFAULT NULL,
  `movie_id` bigint(20) DEFAULT NULL,
  PRIMARY KEY (`id`),
  KEY `FK_MOVIE_ID` (`movie_id`),
  CONSTRAINT `FK_MOVIE_ID`
    FOREIGN KEY (`movie_id`)
    REFERENCES `movie` (`id`)
)
```

Creating the classes

Use the following code to create the classes:

Source file: `Movie.java`

```
@Entity
@Table(name = "movie")
```

```java
public class Movie {

  @Id
  @GeneratedValue
  @Column(name = "id")
  private long id;

  @Column(name = "name")
  private String name;

  @OneToMany(mappedBy = "movie")
  private Set<Actor> actors;

  public long getId() {
    return id;
  }

  public void setId(long id) {
    this.id = id;
  }

  public String getName() {
    return name;
  }

  public void setName(String name) {
    this.name = name;
  }

  public Set<Actor> getActors() {
    return actors;
  }

  public void setActors(Set<Actor> actors) {
    this.actors = actors;
  }

  @Override
  public String toString() {
    return "Movie" + "\n Id: " + this.id +
      "\n Name: " + this.name;

  }
}
```

Source file: `Actor.java`

```java
@Entity
@Table(name = "actor")
public class Actor {

  @Id
  @GeneratedValue
  @Column(name = "id")
  private long id;

  @Column(name = "actorname")
  private String actorName;

  @ManyToOne
  @JoinColumn(name = "movie_id")
  private Movie movie;

  public long getId() {
    return id;
  }

  public void setId(long id) {
    this.id = id;
  }

  public String getActorName() {
    return actorName;
  }

  public void setActorName(String actorName) {
    this.actorName = actorName;
  }

  public Movie getMovie() {
    return movie;
  }

  public void setMovie(Movie movie) {
    this.movie = movie;
  }

  @Override
  public String toString() {
```

```
    return "Actor" + "\n Id: " + this.id +
    "\n Name: " + this.actorName;


  }
}
```

How to do it...

In this section, we will see how to achieve one-to-many or many-to-one associativity using Actor and Movie classes. Also we will learn how to retrieve data from either side i.e. retrieve movie from `actor` and actor from `movie`.

Inserting a record

Use the following code to insert a record, and you will understand how this relationship works:

Code

```
Movie movie= new Movie();
movie.setName("Furious 7");

Actor actor1 = new Actor();
actor1.setActorName("Vin Diesel");
actor1.setMovie(movie);

Actor actor2= new Actor();
actor2.setActorName("Paul Walker");
actor2.setMovie(movie);

Transaction transaction = session.getTransaction();
transaction.begin();
session.save(movie);
session.save(actor1);
session.save(actor2);
transaction.commit();
```

Output

```
Hibernate: insert into movie (name) values (?)
Hibernate: insert into actor (actorname, movie_id) values (?,?)
Hibernate: insert into actor (actorname, movie_id) values (?,?)
```

Retrieving a record – many-to-one-mapping

Here, we will retrieve the `Actor` object and also the `Movie` object associated with it:

Code

```
Criteria criteria = session.createCriteria(Actor.class);
criteria.add(Restrictions.eq("actorName", "Paul Walker"));
Actor actor = (Actor) criteria.uniqueResult();

System.out.println(actor);
System.out.println(actor.getMovie());
```

Output

```
Hibernate: select this_.id as id1_1_, this_.actorname as
actorname1_1_,this_.movie_id as movie3_1_1_, movie2_.id as id0_0_,
movie2_.name as name0_0_ from actor this_ left outer join movie
movie2_ on this_.movie_id=movie2_.id where this_.actorname=?
Actor
 Id: 2
 Name: Paul Walker
Movie
 Id: 1
 Name: Furious 7
```

Retrieving a record – one-to-many-mapping

Now, we will retrieve the `Movie` object and get the `Actor` object associated with that movie:

Code

```
Criteria criteria = session.createCriteria(Movie.class);
criteria.add(Restrictions.eq("id", 1L));
Movie movie = (Movie) criteria.uniqueResult();
System.out.println(movie);

Set<Actor> actors = movie.getActors();
for(Actor actor : actors){
  System.out.println(actor);
}
```

Output

```
Hibernate: select this_.id as id0_0_, this_.name as name0_0_ from
movie this_ where this_.id=?
Movie
 Id: 1
 Name: Furious 7
Hibernate: select actors0_.movie_id as movie3_0_1_, actors0_.id as
id1_, actors0_.id as id1_0_, actors0_.actorname as actorname1_0_,
actors0_.movie_id as movie3_1_0_ from actor actors0_ where
actors0_.movie_id=?
```

```
Actor
  Id: 1
  Name: Vin Diesel
Actor
  Id: 2
  Name: Paul Walker
```

How it works...

From the output, we can easily understand how this relationship works. Let's take a look at an option used in the previous example.

The option from the `Movie` class:

```
@ManyToOne
@JoinColumn(name="movie_id")
private Movie movie;
```

In the preceding code, we used the `@ManyToOne` annotation; it shows many actors associated with one movie. This side of the relationship is considered to be the owning side and is responsible for the update if we use bidirectional operations.

The option from the `Actor` class:

```
@OneToMany(mappedBy = "movie")
private Set<Actor> actors;
```

In the preceding code, we used `mappedBy = "movie"` with the `@OneToMany` annotation; `@OneToMany` shows that one movie is associated with multiple actors, `mappedBy = "movie"` shows that this is the nonowning side of the relationship, and you can get the parent object from the `mappedBy` movie entity.

Many-to-many mapping

This type of relationships seems like an open one, because a record from either side is related to another on the other side. Let's consider one scenario. Here, we will use the `Developer` and `Technology` classes. In this scenario, multiple developers can associate with multiple technologies and vice versa.

Getting ready

Here, we will create the tables and classes to work this demo.

Creating the tables

Use the following script to create the tables if you are not using `hbm2dll=create|update`:

Use the following script to create the `developer` table:

```
CREATE TABLE `developer` (
  `id` bigint(20) NOT NULL AUTO_INCREMENT,
  `name` varchar(255) DEFAULT NULL,
  PRIMARY KEY (`id`)
);
```

Use the following script to create the `technology` table:

```
CREATE TABLE `technology` (
  `id` bigint(20) NOT NULL AUTO_INCREMENT,
  `expertise` varchar(255) DEFAULT NULL,
  `language` varchar(255) DEFAULT NULL,
  PRIMARY KEY (`id`)
);
```

Use the following script to create the `developer_technology` table:

```
CREATE TABLE `developer_technology` (
  `developer_id` bigint(20) NOT NULL,
  `technology_id` bigint(20) NOT NULL,
  PRIMARY KEY (`developer_id`,`technology_id`),
  KEY `FK_TECHNOLOGY_ID` (`technology_id`),
  KEY `FK_DEVELOPER_ID` (`developer_id`),
  CONSTRAINT `FK_DEVELOPER_ID`
    FOREIGN KEY (`developer_id`)
    REFERENCES `developer` (`id`),
  CONSTRAINT `FK_TECHNOLOGY_ID`
    FOREIGN KEY (`technology_id`)
    REFERENCES `technology` (`id`)
);
```

Creating the classes

Use the following code to create the classes:

Source file: `Developer.java`

```
@Entity
@Table(name = "developer")
public class Developer {
  @Id
  @GeneratedValue
```

```java
@Column(name = "id")
private long id;

@Column(name = "name")
private String name;

@ManyToMany(cascade = CascadeType.ALL)
private Set<Technology> technology;

public long getId() {
  return id;
}

public void setId(long id) {
  this.id = id;
}

public String getName() {
  return name;
}

public void setName(String name) {
  this.name = name;
}

public Set<Technology> getTechnology() {
  return technology;
}

public void setTechnology(Set<Technology> technology) {
  this.technology = technology;
}

@Override
public String toString() {
  return "Developer" + "\n Id: " + this.id + "\n Name: " +
this.name;

  }

}
```

Source file: `Technology.java`

```java
@Entity
@Table(name = "technology")
public class Technology {

  @Id
  @GeneratedValue
  @Column(name = "id")
  private long id;

  @Column(name = "language")
  private String language;

  @Column(name = "expertise")
  private String expertise;

  @ManyToMany(mappedBy = "technology")
  private Set<Developer> developer;

  public long getId() {
    return id;
  }

  public void setId(long id) {
    this.id = id;
  }

  public String getLanguage() {
    return language;
  }

  public void setLanguage(String language) {
    this.language = language;
  }

  public String getExpertise() {
    return expertise;
  }

  public void setExpertise(String expertise) {
    this.expertise = expertise;
  }
```

```
    public Set<Developer> getDeveloper() {
      return developer;
    }

    public void setDeveloper(Set<Developer> developer) {
      this.developer = developer;
    }

    @Override
    public String toString() {
      return "Technology"
          +"\n Id: " + this.id
          +"\n Language: " + this.language
          +"\n Expertise: " + this.expertise;


    }


}
```

How to do it...

As a part of the scenario, we will create three `Developer` objects and two `Technology` objects, where all three developers have knowledge on two technologies.

Inserting a record

Here, we will insert three `Developer` and two `Technology` records in to the database. Hibernate will create a mapping between them in a third table. Execute the following code:

Code

```
Developer developer1= new Developer();
developer1.setName("Vishal");

Developer developer2= new Developer();
developer2.setName("Yogesh");

Developer developer3= new Developer();
developer3.setName("Virendra");

Technology technology1=new Technology();
technology1.setLanguage("Java");
technology1.setExpertise("Intermediate");

Technology technology2=new Technology();
```

```
technology2.setLanguage("Bigdata");
technology2.setExpertise("Expert");

Set<Technology> technologies= new HashSet<Technology>();
technologies.add(technology1);
technologies.add(technology2);

developer1.setTechnology(technologies);
developer2.setTechnology(technologies);
developer3.setTechnology(technologies);

Transaction transaction = session.getTransaction();
transaction.begin();
session.save(developer1);
session.save(developer2);
session.save(developer3);
transaction.commit();
```

Output

```
Hibernate: insert into developer (name) values (?)
Hibernate: insert into technology (expertise, language) values
(?,?)
Hibernate: insert into technology (expertise, language) values
(?,?)
Hibernate: insert into developer (name) values (?)
Hibernate: insert into developer (name) values (?)
Hibernate: insert into developer_technology (developer_id,
technology_id) values (?,?)
Hibernate: insert into developer_technology (developer_id,
technology_id) values (?,?)
Hibernate: insert into developer_technology (developer_id,
technology_id) values (?,?)
Hibernate: insert into developer_technology (developer_id,
technology_id) values (?,?)
Hibernate: insert into developer_technology (developer_id,
technology_id) values (?,?)
Hibernate: insert into developer_technology (developer_id,
technology_id) values (?,?)
```

Retrieving a record using Developer with Technology

Here, we will query the Developer object and then try to get all the Technology objects
that Developer knows:

Code

```
Criteria criteria = session.createCriteria(Developer.class);
criteria.add(Restrictions.eq("id", 1L));
```

```
Developer developer = (Developer) criteria.uniqueResult();
System.out.println(developer.toString());

Set<Technology> tech = developer.getTechnology();
for(Technology technology : tech){
  System.out.println(technology.toString());
}
```

Output

```
Hibernate: select this_.id as id0_0_, this_.name as name0_0_ from
developer this_ where this_.id=?
Developer
  Id: 1
  Name: Vishal
Hibernate: select technology0_.developer_id as developer1_0_1_,
technology0_.technology_id as technology2_1_, technology1_.id as
id1_0_, technology1_.expertise as expertise1_0_,
technology1_.language as language1_0_ from developer_technology
technology0_ inner join technology technology1_ on
technology0_.technology_id=technology1_.id where
technology0_.developer_id=?
Technology
  Id: 1
  Language: Java
  Expertise: Intermediate
Technology
  Id: 2
  Language: Bigdata
  Expertise: Expert
```

Retrieving a record using Technology with Developers

Now, we will perform a reverse process; from the Technology object, we will try to get Developers that have knowledge of that Technology. Execute the following code:

Code

```
Criteria criteria = session.createCriteria(Technology.class);
criteria.add(Restrictions.eq("id", 1L));

Technology technology= (Technology) criteria.uniqueResult();

System.out.println(technology);
Set<Developer> devs = technology.getDeveloper();
for(Developer developer : devs){
  System.out.println(developer.toString());
}
```

Output

```
Hibernate: select this_.id as id1_0_, this_.expertise as
expertise1_0_, this_.language as language1_0_ from technology
this_ where this_.id=?
Technology
  Id: 1
  Language: Java
  Expertise: Intermediate
Hibernate: select developer0_.technology_id as technology2_1_1_,
developer0_.developer_id as developer1_1_, developer1_.id as
id0_0_, developer1_.name as name0_0_ from developer_technology
developer0_ inner join developer developer1_ on
developer0_.developer_id=developer1_.id where
developer0_.technology_id=?
Developer
  Id: 2
  Name: Yogesh
Developer
  Id: 3
  Name: Virendra
Developer
  Id: 1
  Name: Vishal
```

How it works...

From the output, we can get information on all the knowledge of technology a particular developer has and also of all the developers who have the knowledge of that particular technology. Execute the following code for their respective options:

The option from `Developer`:

```
@ManyToMany(cascade = CascadeType.ALL)
private Set<Technology> technology;
```

We used the `@ManyToMany` option; it shows that this particular developer can be associated with multiple technologies.

The option from `Technology`:

```
@ManyToMany(mappedBy="technology")
private Set<Developer> developer;
```

We used the `@ManyToMany` option; it shows that this particular technology can be associated with multiple developers. Also, `mappedBy="technology"` shows that this is a nonowning side.

6
Querying

In this chapter, we will cover the following recipes:

- ▸ Working with an alias
- ▸ Performing aggregate operations
- ▸ Executing a subquery using a criteria
- ▸ Executing a native SQL query
- ▸ Executing a query using HQL
- ▸ Using a formula in hibernate
- ▸ Working with NamedQuery

Introduction

This chapter shows a different functionality and an API used to query with hibernate. In this chapter, you will also learn how hibernate provides a facility to perform complex queries in an object-oriented manner.

We will discuss a number of functionalities useful while querying, such as an alias, aggregate functions, and subquery. Sometimes, we need to use a native SQL in hibernate, and you will also learn about executing it. Apart from this, you will learn **HQL (Hibernate Query Language)**, which provides a purely object-oriented way to execute the query, NamedQuery, and formulas.

Working with an alias

An alias is useful when we want a relationship between tables and also when we want to refer to a field of the child object using a field of the parent object. So, an alias works as a bridge between them and is also used to refer to a field.

How to do it...

Let's consider one scenario. We have an `Employee` and `Department` relationship where each employee has only one department, but each department can be used multiple times for different employees. Add the following code to the respective files:

Source file: `Employee.java`

```
@Entity
@Table
public class Employee{

    @Id
    @GeneratedValue
    private long id;

    @Column
    private String name;

    @ManyToOne
    @JoinColumn
    private Department department;

    // getters and setters

}
```

Source file: `Department.java`

```
@Entity
@Table
public class Department{

    @Id
    @GeneratedValue
    private long id;

    @Column
    private String name;

    // getters and setters

}
```

Now, using the criteria of the `Employee` class, we want to access a field `name` of the `Department` class. The following code shows the same.

First, we will take a look at what would happen if we did not use an alias. Execute the following code:

```
Criteria criteria = session.createCriteria(Employee.class);
criteria.add(Restrictions.eq("department.name", "account"));
List list = criteria.list();
```

The preceding code throws an error similar to `could not resolve property: department.name of: Employee`.

Now, to resolve the error, we need to create an alias for the `Department` class. Execute the following code:

```
/* Line 1 */ Criteria criteria =
session.createCriteria(Employee.class);
/* Line 2 */ criteria.createAlias("department", "dept");
/* Line 3 */ criteria.add(Restrictions.eq("dept.name", "account"));
/* Line 4 */ List list = criteria.list();
```

Now it will work as expected.

How it works...

Here, in `Line 2`, we created an alias in the second code snippet. The `createAlias(String, String)` method accepts both the parameters as string: the first is the instance variable of the referenced class (here, the `Department` class), and the other is an alias name (here, `dept`), which will be used further.

In `Line 3`, we used the alias `dept` to refer the `name` field of the `Department` class using the `dept.name` code.

`Line 4` actually makes the call to the database to get the data.

There's more...

Let's consider a department that also refers to another class called `Location`. In this case, let's take a look at how to refer to an attribute of the `Location` class using the criteria of `Employee`. Here, we will create a three-level hierarchy to make the example a bit more complex. Add the following code to the respective files:

Source file: `Location.java`

```
@Entity
@Table
public class Location{
    @Id
    @GeneratedValue
```

```
      private long id;

      @Column
      private String name;
      // getters and setters

   }
```

Source file: `Department.java`

```
   @Entity
   @Table
   public class Department{
     @Id
     @GeneratedValue
     private long id;

     @Column
     private String name;

     @ManyToOne
     @JoinColumn
     private Location location;
     // getters and setters

   }
```

Source file: `Employee.java`

```
   @Entity
   @Table
   public class Employee{
     @Id
     @GeneratedValue
     private long id;

     @Column
     private String name;

     @ManyToOne
     @JoinColumn
     private Department department;
     // getters and setters

   }
```

Let's directly go to the code side:

```
/* Line 1 */ Criteria criteria =
session.createCriteria(Employee.class);

/* Line 3 */ criteria.createAlias("department", "dept");
/* Line 4 */ criteria.createAlias("dept.location", "loc");

/* Line 5 */ criteria.add(Restrictions.eq("loc.name", "AHD"));
List list = criteria.list();
```

Here, we created a chain of aliases to refer to the subclasses. In `Line 3`, we created an alias of the `Department` class, which is `dept`, and in `Line 4`, we created an alias, `"loc"`, which refers to the location class using the previous alias, `"dept"`.

Performing aggregate operations

Next to the common SQL databases, hibernate allows us to perform an aggregate operation using a hibernate API. We can perform an aggregation operation such as `sum`, `avg`, `min`, `max`, `count`, and so on.

We will discuss the use of some aggregate functions by example.

Getting ready

To perform an aggregation operation, we will consider a predefined table structure with the data so that it's easy to understand how the aggregate functions work.

The predefined table and class structure we mentioned earlier can be found in two different classes, `product` and `category`, with their relationship. The following code and script can be used to create a Java class and a database table.

Creating the tables

Use the following script to create the tables if you are not using `hbm2dll=create|update`:

Use the following code to create the `category` table:

```
CREATE TABLE `category` (
  `id` bigint(20) NOT NULL AUTO_INCREMENT,
  `created_on` datetime DEFAULT NULL,
  `name` varchar(255) DEFAULT NULL,
  PRIMARY KEY (`id`)
);
```

Use the following code to create the `product` table:

```
CREATE TABLE `product` (
  `id` bigint(20) NOT NULL AUTO_INCREMENT,
  `name` varchar(255) DEFAULT NULL,
  `price` double DEFAULT NULL,
  `category_id` bigint(20) DEFAULT NULL,
  PRIMARY KEY (`id`),
  KEY `FK_CATEGORY_ID` (`category_id`),
  CONSTRAINT `FK_CATGORY_ID`
FOREIGN KEY (`category_id`)
  REFERENCES `category` (`id`)
);
```

Creating the classes

Use the following code to create the classes:

Source file: `Category.java`

```java
@Entity
@Table(name = "category")
public class Category {

  @Id
  @GeneratedValue
  @Column(name = "id")
  private long id;

  @Column(name = "name")
  private String name;

  @Column(name = "created_on")
  private Date createdOn;

  public long getId() {
    return id;
  }

  public void setId(long id) {
    this.id = id;
  }

  public String getName() {
    return name;
  }
}
```

```java
    public void setName(String name) {
      this.name = name;
    }

    public Date getCreatedOn() {
      return createdOn;
    }

    public void setCreatedOn(Date createdOn) {
      this.createdOn = createdOn;
    }

}
```

Source file: `Product.java`

```java
    @Entity
    @Table(name = "product")
    public class Product {

      @Id
      @GeneratedValue
      @Column(name = "id")
      private long id;

      @Column(name = "name")
      private String name;

      @Column(name = "price")
      private double price;

      @ManyToOne
      @JoinColumn(name = "category_id")
      private Category category;

      public long getId() {
        return id;
      }

      public void setId(long id) {
        this.id = id;
      }

      public String getName() {
        return name;
      }
```

```java
    public void setName(String name) {
      this.name = name;
    }

    public double getPrice() {
      return price;
    }

    public void setPrice(double price) {
      this.price = price;
    }

    public Category getCategory() {
      return category;
    }

    public void setCategory(Category category) {
      this.category = category;
    }

}
```

Inserting data in the tables

We can determine that every product is associated with at least one category. Consider the following table and it's data.

This is the data for the `category` table:

id	created_on	name
1	2015-01-01 15:34:54	Furniture
2	2015-01-22 15:35:02	Stationary

This is the data for the `product` table:

id	name	price	category_id
1	Meeting room table	100.23	1
2	Metal bookcases	120	1
3	Lighting	70.36	1
4	Business envelopes	40.92	2
5	Paper clips	20.61	2
6	Highlighters	30	2

Now for this recipe, we are considering the preceding table structure and data.

How to do it...

Now, we will do the exercise for the different aggregation functions mentioned in the following list using a hibernate API:

- Sum
- Avg
- Min
- Max
- Count

Sum

The aggregate function `sum` is used to obtain the sum of the values of a particular column.

Let's take a look at a scenario where we want the sum of prices by category, and our expected output is as follows:

- Category name: Furniture, Sum of price: 290.59
- Category name: Stationary, Sum of price: 91.53

In this case, execute the following code:

Code

```
Criteria criteria = session.createCriteria(Product.class);
ProjectionList projectionList = Projections.projectionList();
/* Line 4 */projectionList.add(Projections.groupProperty("category"));

/* Line 6 */ projectionList.add(Projections.alias(Projections.
sum("price"),
"price"));
criteria.createAlias("category", "category");
projectionList.add(Projections.alias(Projections.property("categor
y.name"), "cat_name"));

criteria.setProjection(projectionList);
criteria.setResultTransformer(criteria.ALIAS_TO_ENTITY_MAP);

List list = criteria.list();
for (Iterator iterator = list.iterator(); iterator.hasNext();) {
  Map map = (Map) iterator.next();
  System.out.println("Category name: " + map.get("cat_name"));
  System.out.println("SUM(price): " + map.get("price"));
}
```

Output

```
Hibernate: select this_.category_id as y0_, sum(this_.price) as y1_,
category1_.name as y2_ from product this_ inner join category
category1_ on this_.category_id=category1_.id group by
this_.category_id
Hibernate: select category0_.id as id1_0_, category0_.created_on as
created2_1_0_, category0_.name as name1_0_ from category category0_
where category0_.id=?
Hibernate: select category0_.id as id1_0_, category0_.created_on as
created2_1_0_, category0_.name as name1_0_ from category category0_
where category0_.id=?

Category name: Furniture
Sum(price): 290.59000000000003

Category name: Stationary
Sum(price): 91.53
```

The `Projections.sum("price")` code from `Line 6` shows that we wanted the sum of the prices, and the `Projections.groupProperty("category")` code from `Line 4` shows that we used `"category"` as a group property while obtaining the sum of the prices.

Avg

The aggregate function `avg` is used to find the average of values.

Let's consider a scenario where we want the average of the prices by category, and our expected output is as follows:

- ▶ `Category name: Furniture Average of price: 96.86`
- ▶ `Category name: Stationary Average of price: 30.51`

Here, we change a small part of the code in `Line 6` from the sum example; we just change the `Projection.sum(...)` method to `Projection.avg(...)`, as shown in the following code:

Code

```
/* Line 6 */ projectionList.add(Projections.alias(Projections.
avg("price"),
"price"));
```

Output

```
Hibernate: select this_.category_id as y0_, avg(this_.price) as y1_,
category1_.name as y2_ from product this_ inner join category
category1_ on this_.category_id=category1_.id group by
this_.category_id
Hibernate: select category0_.id as id1_0_, category0_.created_on as
created2_1_0_, category0_.name as name1_0_ from category category0_
where category0_.id=?
```

```
Hibernate: select category0_.id as id1_0_, category0_.created_on as
created2_1_0_, category0_.name as name1_0_ from category category0_
where category0_.id=?
```

```
Category name: Furniture
AVG(price): 96.86333333333334
```

```
Category name: Stationary
AVG(price): 30.51
```

Min

The aggregate function `min` is used to find the product having the minimum value in a particular category. Execute the following code:

Code

```
Criteria criteria = session.createCriteria(Product.class);
ProjectionList projectionList = Projections.projectionList();
projectionList.add(Projections.groupProperty("category"));

/* Line 6 */ projectionList.add(Projections.alias(Projections.
min("price"),
"price"));
criteria.createAlias("category", "category");
projectionList.add(Projections.alias(Projections.property("categor
y.name"), "cat_name"));
projectionList.add(Projections.alias(Projections.property("name"),
"prod_name"));

criteria.setProjection(projectionList);
criteria.setResultTransformer(criteria.ALIAS_TO_ENTITY_MAP);

List list = criteria.list();
for (Iterator iterator = list.iterator(); iterator.hasNext();) {
  Map map = (Map) iterator.next();
  System.out.println("\nCategory name: " + map.get("cat_name"));
  System.out.println("Product name: " + map.get("prod_name"));
  System.out.println("MIN(price): " + map.get("price"));
}
```

Output

```
Hibernate: select this_.category_id as y0_, min(this_.price) as y1_,
category1_.name as y2_, this_.name as y3_ from product this_ inner
join
category category1_ on this_.category_id=category1_.id group by
this_.category_id
```

```
Hibernate: select category0_.id as id1_0_, category0_.created_on as
created2_1_0_, category0_.name as name1_0_ from category category0_
where category0_.id=?
Hibernate: select category0_.id as id1_0_, category0_.created_on as
created2_1_0_, category0_.name as name1_0_ from category category0_
where category0_.id=?

Category name: Furniture
Product name: Lighting
MIN(price): 70.36

Category name: Stationary
Product name: Paper clips
MIN(price): 20.61
```

From the output, it's clear that we have a product named `Lighting` in the `Furniture` category that has the minimum price in that category, and product with name `Paper clips` in the `Stationary` category with minimum price in its category.

Max

The aggregate function `max` is used to find the maximum value in a particular category.

Code

Here, we will change a small part of the code in `Line 6` from the *Min* example; we will just change the `Projection.min(…)` method to `Projection.max(…)`, as shown in the following code:

```
/* Line 6 */ projectionList.add(Projections.alias(Projections.
max("price"),
"price"));
```

Output

```
Hibernate: select this_.category_id as y0_, max(this_.price) as y1_,
category1_.name as y2_, this_.name as y3_ from product this_ inner
join
category category1_ on this_.category_id=category1_.id group by
this_.category_id
Hibernate: select category0_.id as id1_0_, category0_.created_on as
created2_1_0_, category0_.name as name1_0_ from category category0_
where category0_.id=?
Hibernate: select category0_.id as id1_0_, category0_.created_on as
created2_1_0_, category0_.name as name1_0_ from category category0_
where category0_.id=?

Category name: Furniture Product
name: Meeting room table
MAX(price): 120.0
```

```
Category name: Stationary
Product name: Business envelopes
MAX(price): 40.92
```

Count

The aggregate function `count` is used to count the number of occurrences of a value.

Code

Here again, we will change a small part of the code in `Line 6` from the *Max* example; we will just change the `Projection.max(...)` method to `Projection.cont(...)`, as shown in the following code:

```
/* Line 6 */ projectionList.add(Projections.alias(Projections.
count("price"),
"price"));
```

Output

```
Hibernate: select this_.category_id as y0_, count(this_.price) as y1_,
category1_.name as y2_, this_.name as y3_ from product this_ inner
join
category category1_ on this_.category_id=category1_.id group by
this_.category_id
Hibernate: select category0_.id as id1_0_, category0_.created_on as
created2_1_0_, category0_.name as name1_0_ from category category0_
where category0_.id=?
Hibernate: select category0_.id as id1_0_, category0_.created_on as
created2_1_0_, category0_.name as name1_0_ from category category0_
where category0_.id=?

Category name: Furniture
COUNT(price): 3

Category name: Stationary
COUNT(price): 3
```

From the output, it's clear that we have three products in each category.

 count only calculates the number of records. If you need a distinct count of the values, another method available is as follows:

```
Projections.countDistinct(String propertyName);
```

Executing a subquery using a criteria

In this recipe, we will take a look at how to use subquery. Here, we will do the same thing as before; we will use the `DetachedCriteria` class provided by the hibernate API. The `DetachedCriteria` class works in `detached mode` and is used to create a criteria query when the session is not available, as we can execute `DetachedCriteria` with the existing session object.

How to do it...

We will create one scenario to show how `DetachedCriteria` acts as a subquery.

The scenario is to get all the products whose categories have been recently added.

The preferred solution for this problem is as follows:

► First, we will create `DetachedCriteria` to find the maximum `createdOn` date

► Then, we will use the result of the first query to check the date of the product's category

Consider the following code:

Code

```
/* Line 1 */ DetachedCriteria detachedCriteria =
DetachedCriteria.forClass(Category.class);
/* Line 2 */
detachedCriteria.setProjection(Projections.max("createdOn"));

/* Line 4 */ Criteria criteria =
session.createCriteria(Product.class);
/* Line 5 */ criteria.createAlias("category", "cat");
/* Line 6 */ criteria.add(Subqueries.propertyEq("cat.createdOn",
detachedCriteria));
List<Product> list = criteria.list();
for(Product product : list){
  System.out.println("\nProduct id: " + product.getId());
  System.out.println("Product name: " + product.getName());
  System.out.println("Product price: " + product.getPrice());
  System.out.println("Category name: " +
  product.getCategory().getName());
}
```

```
Hibernate: select this_.id as id0_1_, this_.category_id as
category4_0_1_, this_.name as name0_1_, this_.price as price0_1_,
cat1_.id as id1_0_, cat1_.created_on as created2_1_0_, cat1_.name as
name1_0_ from product this_ inner join category cat1_ on
this_.category_id=cat1_.id where cat1_.created_on = (select
max(this_.created_on) as y0_ from category this_)

Product id: 4
Product name: Business envelopes
Product price: 40.92
Category name: Stationary

Product id: 5
Product name: Paper clips
Product price: 20.61
Category name: Stationary

Product id: 6
Product name: Highlighters
Product price: 30.0
Category name: Stationary
```

How it works...

From the output, it's clear that we have the last inserted category, which is Stationary; so, we got all the products under the Stationary category.

Line 1 and 2 from the preceding code show that we want to create a DetachedCriteria object for the Category class. Here, the task of DetachedCriteria is to find the maximum createdOn date from the category table.

In Line 4, we created the Criteria object for the Product class. In Line 6, we passed an object of DetachedCriteria in the SubQueries object, so hibernate will create a subquery for DetachedCriteria.

Executing a native SQL query

We can directly use a hand-written core SQL query with hibernate. This is a useful feature if we want to execute a database-specific query that is not supported by the hibernate API, such as query hints or the CONNECT keyword in an Oracle database.

This is a useful feature when the developer has a ready native SQL. We can perform the Select, non-select, and Bulk operations as well.

How to do it...

We can use `Session.createSQLQuery(String query)` to execute a SQL query. We have multiple APIs available to execute the SQL query, and we will take a look at these in detail:

- ▶ Scalar queries
- ▶ Entity queries

Scalar queries

This is a basic type of query that returns a list of values (scalar).

For example, the following code shows how to select all the products from the product table:

Code

```
SQLQuery sqlQuery = session.createSQLQuery("SELECT * FROM product");

List<Object[]> list = sqlQuery.list();
for(Object[] object : list){
  System.out.println("\nId: " + object[0]);
  System.out.println("Name: " + object[1]);
  System.out.println("Price: " + object[2]);
  System.out.println("Category id: " + object[3]);
}
```

Output

```
Hibernate: SELECT * FROM product

Id: 1
Name: Meeting room table
Price: 100.23
Category id: 1

Id: 2
Name: Metal bookcases
Price: 120.0
Category id: 1

Id: 3
Name: Lighting
Price: 70.36
Category id: 1

Id: 4
Name: Business envelopes
```

```
Price: 40.92
Category id: 2


Id: 5
Name: Paper clips
Price: 20.61
Category id: 2


Id: 6
Name: Highlighters
Price: 30.0
Category id: 2
```

We can understand from the output that hibernate directly uses the query that is provided by us.

Here, we used the `SELECT * FROM product` query, which is equivalent to `SELECT id, name, price, category_id FROM product`, with which it would select all four fields from the product table. So, we can get `Object []` of size 4. Hibernate returns `List` of `Object` array (`List<Object[]>`).

When we use this methodology to execute a SQL query, hibernate uses `ResultSetMetadata` to determine the order and data type of the fields. So, it will create an overhead for hibernate to get the field detail. To remove this overhead from hibernate, we can use the `addScalar(String fieldName, Type dataType)` method in the following way:

```
SQLQuery sqlQuery = session.createSQLQuery("SELECT id, name, price,
category_id FROM product");
sqlQuery.addScalar("id", new org.hibernate.type.LongType());
sqlQuery.addScalar("name", new org.hibernate.type.StringType());
sqlQuery.addScalar("price", new org.hibernate.type.DoubleType());
sqlQuery.addScalar("category_id", new
org.hibernate.type.LongType());
sqlQuery.setResultTransformer(Transformers.ALIAS_TO_ENTITY_MAP);
List list = sqlQuery.list();
```

Here, we defined a data type for each field using the `addScalar(...)` method. Another thing to add here is that we used `ResultsetTransformers` to transform the result to `Map`. So, now it returns a `List` of `Map` (`List<Map>`).

Entity queries

In the previous section, we went through the scalar queries, which always return a list of values, and we have to iterate all the values horizontally and vertically, which means over rows and columns. It is useful to remove this iteration from our (developer) end `Entity` query. The `Entity` query automatically fills an entity from the values returned by the query.

Here, as a part of our recipe, we will execute the following query to select all the products from the table and get the returned data into the `Product` entity:

Code

```
SQLQuery sqlQuery = session.createSQLQuery("SELECT * FROM category");
/* Line 2 */ sqlQuery.addEntity(Category.class);

List<Category> list = sqlQuery.list();
for(Category category: list){
System.out.println("\nCategory id: " + category.getId());
System.out.println("Category name: " + category.getName());
}
```

Output

```
Hibernate: SELECT * FROM category

Category id: 1
Category name: Furniture

Category id: 2
Category name: Stationary
```

Here, we used the `addEntity(Class className)` method to add the entity. Here, we added the `Category.class` to add the entity shown in `Line 2`.

Executing a query using HQL

HQL stands for Hibernate Query Language and is a fully object-oriented language. This language is a bit similar to the native query, but in the native SQL query, we use the physical table name and actual physical columns to execute a query, and in HQL, we have to use a class name instead of a table name and a field name instead of a column name.

HQL queries are converted to SQL queries by hibernate; so, we can use any of the styles. However, HQL is preferable from a performance point of view, because hibernate uses SQL directly without any optimization, and the HQL query uses hibernate's query generation strategy and caching mechanism.

How to do it...

There are multiple clauses available to work with HQL.

The FROM clause

We will use the simple `FROM` clause to query an object to load the complete object.

Here, we will use the `FROM Category` query, which is equal to `SELECT * FROM category` in native SQL. Execute the following code:

Code

```
Query query = session.createQuery("FROM Category");
List<Category> list = query.list();
System.out.println("Category size: " + list.size());
```

Output

```
Hibernate: select category0_.id as id1_, category0_.created_on as
created2_1_, category0_.name as name1_ from category category0_
Category size: 2
```

From the output, it's clear that hibernate will execute a complete `SELECT` statement for the `Category` class for the `FROM Category` query.

 In HQL statements, the class name, used instead of the table, and fields, used instead of the columns, are case-sensitive; we can use the other part of the query in any case. For example, we can use `fRoM` or `From` instead of `FROM`.

We can use multiple classes in the same query, which results in a Cartesian product or cross join.

Execute the following code:

Code

```
Query query = session.createQuery("FroM Category, Product");
List list = query.list();
System.out.println("Result size: " + list.size());
```

Output

```
Hibernate: select category0_.id as id1_0_, product1_.id as id0_1_,
category0_.created_on as created2_1_0_, category0_.name as name1_0_,
product1_.category_id as category4_0_1_, product1_.name as name0_1_,
product1_.price as price0_1_ from category category0_ cross join
product product1_
Result size: 12
```

Here, we used two classes: the first is `Category` and the other is `Product`. We have two records in the `category` table and six records in the `product` table, so the resulting size is 12, which is equal to a *Cartesian product (6 * 2 = 12)*. This query returns a `List` of `Object` array (`List<Object[]>`).

We can use an alias to refer to this class in another part of the query, as shown in the following code:

```
String hql = "FROM Category c, Product p WHERE c.id=1";
```

The SELECT clause

The FROM clause used in the preceding section selects all the fields from a given class. SELECT is used when we need limited columns.

Execute the following code:

Code

```
Query query = session.createQuery("SELECT id, name from Category");
List list = query.list();
System.out.println("Result size: " + list.size());
```

Output

```
Hibernate: select category0_.id as col_0_0_, category0_.name as
col_1_0_ from category category0_
Result size: 2
```

Here, hibernate creates a SQL query with only two fields, which is given in HQL.

How it works...

When we use HQL, hibernate internally creates SQL. Hibernate uses the mapping provided via an HBM file if it is an XML-based mapping and uses annotations if it is an annotation-based mapping to convert HQL into a SQL query.

Hibernate uses a query generation strategy and caching mechanism in the HQL query. Query generation is used while converting HQL to SQL, and caching is used after the query execution is complete.

There's more...

In this section, we will demonstrate the use of the FROM and SELECT clauses. But apart from these clauses, we can also use the other SQL clauses, as shown in the following examples:

The WHERE clause

Here is an example:

```
String hql = "FROM Category c WHERE c.id=1";
```

The ORDER BY clause

Here is an example:

```
String hql = "FROM Category c ORDER BY c.id DESC";
```

The GROUP BY clause

Here is an example:

```
String hql = "SELECT COUNT(p.id), p.name FROM Product p GROUP BY
p.category";
```

Apart from this, we can use subquery, joins, named queries, and expressions such as mathematical, logical, comparison, Update, and Delete.

Using formula in hibernate

Sometimes, we need a calculated column in hibernate; at such a time, the formula feature is used. For this, we will use the @Formula annotation with the field.

The field annotated with the @Formula annotation is a read-only field, and the formula is only applied while using the SELECT operation.

How to do it...

To show how formula works, we will change a Product class and add a field, capitalName, which has no physical column in the product table, as shown in the following code:

Source file: Product.java

```
@Entity
@Table(name = "product")
public class Product {

    @Id
    @GeneratedValue
    @Column(name = "id")
    private long id;

    @Column(name = "name")
    private String name;

    @Formula("UPPER(name)")
    private String capitalName;

    @Column(name = "price")
```

```
    private double price;

    @ManyToOne
    @JoinColumn(name = "category_id")
    private Category category;

    // Getters and setters
}
```

Now, we will run a code to show how it works:

Code

```
Criteria criteria = session.createCriteria(Product.class);
List<Product> list = criteria.list();
for(Product product : list){
  System.out.println("\nProduct name: " + product.getName());
  System.out.println("Product capital name: " +
product.getCapitalName());
}
```

Output

```
Hibernate: select this_.id as id0_1_, this_.category_id as
category4_0_1_, this_.name as name0_1_, this_.price as price0_1_,
UPPER(this_.name) as formula0_1_, category2_.id as id1_0_,
category2_.created_on as created2_1_0_, category2_.name as name1_0_
from product this_ left outer join category category2_ on
this_.category_id=category2_.id

Product name: Meeting room table
Product capital name: MEETING ROOM TABLE

Product name: Metal bookcases
Product capital name: METAL BOOKCASES

Product name: Lighting
Product capital name: LIGHTING

Product name: Business envelopes
Product capital name: BUSINESS ENVELOPES

Product name: Paper clips
Product capital name: PAPER CLIPS

Product name: Highlighters
Product capital name: HIGHLIGHTERS
```

How it works...

Hibernate uses the phrase provided in `@Formula` directly in the SQL query. In the formula, we can use any SQL clause supported by the database.

From the output, we can easily understand that hibernate uses the string which is given in `@Formula` annotation in a similar way to `UPPER(this_.name)`.

There's more...

Here, we will take a smaller example to convert a product name to uppercase. Apart from this, we can use all the SQL clauses in the formula. Now, we will use a whole query in the formula.

For this, we will add one more field, named `categoryName`, in the product class to fetch the category name. Execute the following code:

Source file: `Category.java`

```
@Entity
@Table(name = "product")
public class Product {

  @Formula("(SELECT c.name FROM category c WHERE c.id=category_id)")
  private String categoryName;

  // Other fields and getters/setters
}
```

Code

```
Criteria criteria = session.createCriteria(Product.class);
List<Product> list = criteria.list();
for(Product product : list){
  System.out.println("\nProduct name: " + product.getName());
  System.out.println("Category name: " +
product.getCategoryName());
}
```

Output

```
Hibernate: select this_.id as id0_1_, this_.category_id as
category4_0_1_, this_.name as name0_1_, this_.price as price0_1_,
UPPER(this_.name) as formula0_1_, (SELECT c.name FROM category c WHERE
c.id=this_.category_id) as formula1_1_, category2_.id as id1_0_,
category2_.created_on as created2_1_0_, category2_.name as name1_0_
from product this_ left outer join category category2_ on
this_.category_id=category2_.id
```

```
Product name: Meeting room table
Category name: Furniture

Product name: Metal bookcases
Category name: Furniture

Product name: Lighting
Category name: Furniture

Product name: Business envelopes
Category name: Stationary

Product name: Paper clips
Category name: Stationary

Product name: Highlighters
Category name: Stationary
```

From the output, we understand that hibernate will use our query provided in `@Formula` as a subquery.

Working with NamedQuery

NamedQuery is another useful feature provided by hibernate. Sometimes, we require a query or a bunch of queries multiple times in the life of an application; at such a time, this feature helps.

How to do it...

Let's create a scenario to understand this feature.

Let's consider that we want to search a category by name. The following code shows how NamedQuery would help us in this case.

For this, we will use the `@NamedQuery` and `@NamedQueries` annotations in a class:

- ▶ `@NamedQuery`: This annotation is used to define a single named query
- ▶ `@NamedQueries`: This annotation is used to define multiple queries

Update the following code in their respective files:

Source file: `Category.java`

```
@NamedQuery(name="getCategoryNameByName", query="FROM Category c
WHERE c.name=:name")
```

```
@Entity
@Table(name = "category")
public class Category {

    // fields and getters/setters
}
```

Here, we defined NamedQuery using the @NamedQuery annotation, and we used two attributes.

name

The name attribute accepts string, which helps to identify NamedQuery. For example: name="getCategoryNameByName".

query

The query attribute accepts string. This defines a query, which can be either SQL or HQL. For example: query="FROM Category c WHERE c.name=:name".

Take a look at the following code:

Code

```
/* Line 1 */ Query query =
session.getNamedQuery("getCategoryNameByName");
/* Line 2 */ query.setString("name", "Stationary");
List list = query.list();
System.out.println("Category size: " + list.size());
```

Output

```
Hibernate: select category0_.id as id1_, category0_.created_on as
created2_1_, category0_.name as name1_ from category category0_ where
category0_.name=?
Category size: 1
```

We can determine from the output that hibernate will get a query using the name parameter shown in Line 1. We set a named parameter, "name", using the setString(...) method shown in Line 2.

> The value in the name parameter should be unique to the application. If hibernate finds a value of a parameter multiple times, it will throw an error. This is similar to "Duplicate query mapping getCategoryNameByName", if the name getCategoryNameByName were defined multiple times in an application.

There's more...

Now, let's take a look at how to use @NamedQueries to define multiple NamedQueries.

In the previous section, we created NamedQuery for "getCategoryNameByName". Now, we need one more query, such as "getCategoryNameById". Let's take a look at how to define it:

Source file: Category.java

```
@NamedQueries(
    {
      @NamedQuery(
        name="getCategoryNameByName",
        query="FROM Category c WHERE c.name=:name"
      ),
      @NamedQuery(
        name="getCategoryNameById",
        query="FROM Category c WHERE c.id=:id"
      ),
    }
)

@Entity
@Table(name = "category")
public class Category {

    // fields and getters/setters
}
```

This works in the same way as @NamedQuery. This is only used to define multiple NamedQueries.

7
Advanced Concepts

In this chapter, we will cover the following recipes:

- ▶ Working with a first-level cache
- ▶ Working with a second-level cache
- ▶ Working with a query cache
- ▶ Working with the table per class hierarchy strategy of inheritance
- ▶ Working with the table per subclass strategy of inheritance
- ▶ Working with the table per concrete class strategy of inheritance
- ▶ Working with the versioning of objects
- ▶ Maintaining the history of an object
- ▶ Working with an interceptor
- ▶ Working with batch processing

Introduction

Hibernate supports some advanced features, such as caching, inheritance, versioning, maintaining a history of objects, interceptor, batch processing, and many more.

Here, you will learn the first-level, second-level, and query caches, in detail and with an example, to see how to cache particular objects and how caching works. Apart from this, you will also learn a useful feature of hibernate called inheritance, which hibernate provides as a facility to be applied on the database side. You will learn three major inheritance types in this chapter. We will also will look into versioning, maintaining a history of data or of an object for a sensitive application, and at last, how to intercept hibernate's processing and how to perform batch processing using hibernate.

Working with a first-level cache

Once we execute a particular query using hibernate, it always hits the database. As this process may be very expensive, hibernate provides the facility to cache objects within a certain boundary.

The basic actions performed in each database transaction are as follows:

1. The request reaches the database server via the network.
2. The database server processes the query in the query plan.
3. Now the database server executes the processed query.
4. Again, the database server returns the result to the querying application through the network.
5. At last, the application processes the results.

This process is repeated every time we request a database operation, even if it is for a simple or small query. It is always a costly transaction to hit the database for the same records multiple times. Sometimes, we also face some delay in receiving the results because of network routing issues. There may be some other parameters that affect and contribute to the delay, but network routing issues play a major role in this cycle.

To overcome this issue, the database uses a mechanism that stores the result of a query, which is executed repeatedly, and uses this result again when the data is requested using the same query. These operations are done on the database side. Hibernate provides an in-built caching mechanism known as the first-level cache (L1 cache).

Following are some properties of the first-level cache:

▶ It is enabled by default. We cannot disable it even if we want to.

▶ The scope of the first-level cache is limited to a particular `Session` object only; the other `Session` objects cannot access it.

▶ All cached objects are destroyed once the session is closed.

▶ If we request for an object, hibernate returns the object from the cache only if the requested object is found in the cache; otherwise, a database call is initiated.

▶ We can use `Session.evict(Object object)` to remove single objects from the session cache.

▶ The `Session.clear()` method is used to clear all the cached objects from the session.

Getting ready

Let's take a look at how the L1 cache works.

Creating the classes

For this recipe, we will create an `Employee` class and also insert some records into the table:

Source file: `Employee.java`

```java
@Entity
@Table
public class Employee {

  @Id
  @GeneratedValue
  private long id;

  @Column(name = "name")
  private String name;

  // getters and setters

  @Override
  public String toString() {
    return "Employee: " +
        "\n\t Id: " + this.id +
        "\n\t Name: " + this.name;
  }
}
```

Creating the tables

Use the following table script if the `hibernate.hbm2ddl.auto` configuration property is not set to `create`:

Use the following script to create the `employee` table:

```sql
CREATE TABLE `employee` (
  `id` bigint(20) NOT NULL AUTO_INCREMENT,
  `name` varchar(255) DEFAULT NULL,
  PRIMARY KEY (`id`)
);
```

We will assume that two records are already inserted, as shown in the following `employee` table:

id	name
1	Yogesh
2	Aarush

Now, let's take a look at some scenarios that show how the first-level cache works.

How to do it...

Here is the code to see how caching works. In the code, we will load `employee#1` and `employee#2` once; after that, we will try to load the same employees again and see what happens:

Code

```
System.out.println("\nLoading employee#1...");
/* Line 2 */ Employee employee1 = (Employee)
session.load(Employee.class, new Long(1));
System.out.println(employee1.toString());

System.out.println("\nLoading employee#2...");
/* Line 6 */ Employee employee2 = (Employee)
session.load(Employee.class, new Long(2));
System.out.println(employee2.toString());

System.out.println("\nLoading employee#1 again...");
/* Line 10 */ Employee employee1_dummy = (Employee)
session.load(Employee.class, new Long(1));
System.out.println(employee1_dummy.toString());

System.out.println("\nLoading employee#2 again...");
/* Line 15 */ Employee employee2_dummy = (Employee)
session.load(Employee.class, new Long(2));
System.out.println(employee2_dummy.toString());
```

Output

```
Loading employee#1...
Hibernate: select employee0_.id as id0_0_, employee0_.name as
name0_0_ from Employee employee0_ where employee0_.id=?
Employee:
  Id: 1
```

```
   Name: Yogesh

Loading employee#2...
Hibernate: select employee0_.id as id0_0_, employee0_.name as
name0_0_ from Employee employee0_ where employee0_.id=?
Employee:
  Id: 2
  Name: Aarush

Loading employee#1 again...
Employee:
  Id: 1
  Name: Yogesh

Loading employee#2 again...
Employee:
  Id: 2
  Name: Aarush
```

How it works...

Here, we loaded `Employee#1` and `Employee#2` as shown in `Line 2` and `6` respectively and also the print output for both. It's clear from the output that hibernate will hit the database to load `Employee#1` and `Employee#2` because at startup, no object is cached in hibernate. Now, in `Line 10`, we tried to load `Employee#1` again. At this time, hibernate did not hit the database but simply use the cached object because `Employee#1` is already loaded and this object is still in the session. The same thing happened with `Employee#2`.

Hibernate stores an object in the cache only if one of the following operations is completed:

- ► Save
- ► Update
- ► Get
- ► Load
- ► List

There's more...

In the previous section, we took a look at how caching works. Now, we will discuss some other methods used to remove a cached object from the session.

There are two more methods that are used to remove a cached object:

- ▶ `evict(Object object)`: This method removes a particular object from the session
- ▶ `clear()`: This method removes all the objects from the session

evict (Object object)

This method is used to remove a particular object from the session. It is very useful. The object is no longer available in the session once this method is invoked and the request for the object hits the database:

Code

```
System.out.println("\nLoading employee#1...");
/* Line 2 */ Employee employee1 = (Employee)
session.load(Employee.class, new Long(1));
System.out.println(employee1.toString());

/* Line 5 */ session.evict(employee1);
System.out.println("\nEmployee#1 removed using evict(…)...");

System.out.println("\nLoading employee#1 again...");
/* Line 9*/ Employee employee1_dummy = (Employee)
session.load(Employee.class, new Long(1));
System.out.println(employee1_dummy.toString());
```

Output

```
Loading employee#1...
Hibernate: select employee0_.id as id0_0_, employee0_.name as
name0_0_ from Employee employee0_ where employee0_.id=?
Employee:
  Id: 1
  Name: Yogesh

Employee#1 removed using evict(…)...

Loading employee#1 again...
Hibernate: select employee0_.id as id0_0_, employee0_.name as
name0_0_ from Employee employee0_ where employee0_.id=?
Employee:
  Id: 1
  Name: Yogesh
```

Here, we loaded an `Employee#1`, as shown in `Line 2`. This object was then cached in the session, but we explicitly removed it from the session cache in `Line 5`. So, the loading of `Employee#1` will again hit the database.

clear()

This method is used to remove all the cached objects from the session cache. They will no longer be available in the session once this method is invoked and the request for the objects hits the database:

Code

```
System.out.println("\nLoading employee#1...");
/* Line 2 */ Employee employee1 = (Employee)
session.load(Employee.class, new Long(1));
System.out.println(employee1.toString());

System.out.println("\nLoading employee#2...");
/* Line 6 */ Employee employee2 = (Employee)
session.load(Employee.class, new Long(2));
System.out.println(employee2.toString());

/* Line 9 */ session.clear();
System.out.println("\nAll objects removed from session cache using
clear()...");

System.out.println("\nLoading employee#1 again...");
/* Line 13 */ Employee employee1_dummy = (Employee)
session.load(Employee.class, new Long(1));
System.out.println(employee1_dummy.toString());

System.out.println("\nLoading employee#2 again...");
/* Line 17 */ Employee employee2_dummy = (Employee)
session.load(Employee.class, new Long(2));
System.out.println(employee2_dummy.toString());
```

Output

```
Loading employee#1...
Hibernate: select employee0_.id as id0_0_, employee0_.name as
name0_0_ from Employee employee0_ where employee0_.id=?
Employee:
  Id: 1
  Name: Yogesh

Loading employee#2...
Hibernate: select employee0_.id as id0_0_, employee0_.name as
name0_0_ from Employee employee0_ where employee0_.id=?
Employee:
  Id: 2
  Name: Aarush
```

```
All objects removed from session cache using clear()...

Loading employee#1 again...
Hibernate: select employee0_.id as id0_0_, employee0_.name as
name0_0_ from Employee employee0_ where employee0_.id=?
Employee:
  Id: 1
  Name: Yogesh

Loading employee#2 again...
Hibernate: select employee0_.id as id0_0_, employee0_.name as
name0_0_ from Employee employee0_ where employee0_.id=?
Employee:
  Id: 2
  Name: Aarush
```

Here, `Line` 2 and 6 show how to load `Employee#1` and `Employee#2` respectively. Now, we removed all the objects from the session cache using the `clear()` method. As a result, the loading of both `Employee#1` and `Employee#2` will again result in a database hit, as shown in `Line` 13 and 17.

Working with a second-level cache

In the previous section, you learned about the first-level cache, which is enabled by default and whose scope is limited to a particular session.

Now, the scope of the second-level cache is `SessionFactory`, and we can use the cached objects across the different sessions that are created using this particular `SessionFactory`. Hibernate provides the option to either enable or disable the second-level cache.

Hibernate provides a facility to change the cache provider, which means that we can provide any cache provider that supports integration with hibernate. **Ehcache** is used as the default cache provider by hibernate. Apart from Ehcache, there are some other providers available that support integration with hibernate. They are listed as follows:

▶ OSCache

▶ SwarmCache

▶ JBoss Cache

In this recipe, we will consider integration with Ehcache.

Getting ready

For this recipe to be successful, we need one more JAR file for Ehcache. We can download the Ehcache distribution from the official site, `http://ehcache.org/downloads/`. You can use the following Maven configuration for a Maven-based project:

```
<dependency>
    <groupId>net.sf.ehcache</groupId>
    <artifactId>ehcache-core</artifactId>
    <version>2.6.9</version>
</dependency>

<dependency>
    <groupId>org.hibernate</groupId>
    <artifactId>hibernate-ehcache</artifactId>
    <version>4.3.5.Final</version>
</dependency>
```

Enabling a second-level cache

We need to change the configuration.

To enable the second-level cache, we need to add two new mappings in the configuration (CFG) file.

The mappings are as follows:

```
<property name="hibernate.cache.use_second_level_cache">
  true
</property>
<property name="hibernate.cache.region.factory_class">
  net.sf.ehcache.hibernate.EhCacheRegionFactory
</property>
```

The first `property` tag is used to enable the second-level cache. We must set the value of the `hibernate.cache.use_second_level_cache` property to `true`.

Another tag is used to provide a cache provider class, which is vendor-specific. Here, we will set the value of the `hibernate.cache.region.factory_class` property to `net.sf.ehcache.hibernate.EhCacheRegionFactory` as we will use Ehcache here.

Adding a caching strategy using a POJO class

We need to explicitly state which class needs to be cached using the second-level cache and which strategy is to be used for this:

Source file: `Employee.java`

```
@Entity
@Table(name="employee")
@Cache(usage=CacheConcurrencyStrategy.READ_ONLY)
public class Employee {
    // fields and getters/setters
}
```

Here, we used the `@Cache` annotation on top of the `Employee` class to inform hibernate that the result of this class should be cached if any transaction is made for this class.

The `usage` attribute is used to provide a caching strategy. We can provide five caching strategies, which are defined in `enum CacheConcurrencyStrategy`:

- ▶ `CacheConcurrencyStrategy.READ_ONLY`: This strategy is suitable where the data never changes but is required frequently.

- ▶ `CacheConcurrencyStrategy.NONSTRICT_READ_WRITE`: This strategy is suitable for the applications that only rarely need to modify data.

- ▶ `CacheConcurrencyStrategy.READ_WRITE`: This strategy is suitable for the applications that regularly need to modify data.

- ▶ `CacheConcurrencyStrategy.TRNSACTIONAL`: The transactional cache strategy provides support to transactional cache providers such as JBoss TreeCache.

How to do it...

Now we will consider a basic example of the `READ_ONLY` caching strategy. Consider the following code:

Code

```
/* Line 1*/ Session session = sessionFactory.openSession();
/* Line 2 */ Employee employee = (Employee) session.load(Employee.
class, new Long(1));
System.out.println(employee.toString());
/* Line 4 */ session.close();

/* Line 6 */ Session anotherSession = sessionFactory.openSession();
/* Line 7 */ Employee employee_dummy = (Employee) anotherSession.
load(Employee.class, new Long(1));
System.out.println(employee_dummy.toString());
/* Line 9 */ anotherSession.close();
```

Output

```
Hibernate: select employee0_.id as id0_0_, employee0_.name as
name0_0_ from employee employee0_ where employee0_.id=?
Employee:
  Id: 1
  Name: Yogesh
Employee:
  Id: 1
  Name: Yogesh
```

How it works...

We will now take a look at how the second-level cache works with reference to the preceding code. Here, we opened a session to load `Employee#1` in `Line 1`, and this session was closed in `Line 4` after the loading was complete. Next, we opened a new session in `Line 6` and tried to load the same `Employee` object. It's clear from the output that the object was loaded from the cache because in a first-level caching, objects are destroyed when the session is closed. However, here we got the same object without hitting the database.

The flow of a second-level caching is as follows:

1. When hibernate tries to load a particular entity, it first looks for the first-level cache of the current session.

2. It is returned if the requested entity is present in the first-level cache.

3. If this particular entity is not found in the first-level cache, it will look for the second-level cache.

4. If the entity is found in the second-level cache, it's returned. Hibernate also stores this entity in the particular session, so there is no need to go to the second-level cache on the next request.

5. If the entity is not found in the second-level cache, hibernate hits the database and stores it in both the first and second-level caches and then returns it.

Working with a query cache

Hibernate supports a useful feature that actually helps to improve the performance of the application by reducing the processing time. The feature we are talking about here is called **query cache**.

Hibernate caches the query result, which is frequently used. This feature is only useful if the same queries are executed frequently.

Getting ready

To understand the query cache, we will use the `Employee` POJO that was created in the previous recipe entitled *Working with a first-level cache*. We also need to modify `hibernate.cfg.xml` to enable the query cache feature:

Source file: `Employee.java`

```
@Entity
public class Employee {

    @Id
    @GeneratedValue
    private long id;

    @Column(name = "name")
    private String name;

    // getters and setters

}
```

Enabling a query cache:

To use this feature, we will first need to enable the query cache by adding the following tag in the configuration file:

```
<property name="hibernate.cache.use_query_cache">true</property>
```

How to do it...

Here, we will create an executable class to see how the query cache works. The following code shows the same:

```
Session session = sessionFactory.openSession();
for (int i = 0; i < 5; i++) {
    /* Line 3 */ Criteria criteria =
session.createCriteria(Employee.class).setCacheable(true);
    List<Employee> employees = criteria.list();
    System.out.println("Employees found: " + employees.size());
}
session.close();
```

The following is the output for the preceding code:

```
Hibernate: select this_.id as id0_0_, this_.name as name0_0_ from
employee this_
Employees found: 1
Employees found: 1
Employees found: 1
Employees found: 1
Employees found: 1
```

How it works...

In the preceding code, we executed the same query five times using a loop. This means that the query should hit the database five times in order to search. But as shown in output, it hits the database only once and from the second time onward, hibernate checks whether this particular query is cached or not. If the query is found in the cache, it just displays the output; if it's not found in the cache, it first adds it to cache and executes it against the database and then displays the result.

From the output, it looks similar to the first-level cache, but there is actually a difference between the two of them. The query cache checks whether a particular query is cached or not and the first-level cache checks the object in this particular cache. An invocation of the `list()` method always hits the database even if the first-level cache is enabled.

As shown in `Line 3`, we used the `setCachable(true)` method. Once we set `cachable` to `true`, it tells hibernate to cache the particular query.

There's more...

Let's take a look at what happens if we ignore the `setCachable(…)` method. Consider the following code:

Code

```
Session session = sessionFactory.openSession();
for (int i = 0; i < 5; i++) {
  /* Line 3 */ Criteria criteria =
session.createCriteria(Employee.class);
  List<Employee> employees = criteria.list();
  System.out.println("Employees found: " + employees.size());
}
session.close();
```

Output

```
Hibernate: select this_.id as id0_0_, this_.name as name0_0_ from
employee this_
Employees found: 1
Hibernate: select this_.id as id0_0_, this_.name as name0_0_ from
employee this_
Employees found: 1
Hibernate: select this_.id as id0_0_, this_.name as name0_0_ from
employee this_
Employees found: 1
Hibernate: select this_.id as id0_0_, this_.name as name0_0_ from
employee this_
Employees found: 1
Hibernate: select this_.id as id0_0_, this_.name as name0_0_ from
employee this_
Employees found: 1
```

From the output, it's clear that if we don't set `setcachable` to `true`, hibernate will not cache our query, and the query will hit the database every time the loop iterates. This is not a feasible option as it may downgrade the performance.

Working with the table per class hierarchy strategy of inheritance

Java is an object-oriented programming language, and while working with the object-oriented paradigm, one thing comes to our mind: inheritance. We form a real-world scenario using IS A and HAS A relationships. Inheritance is supported by many languages, but relational databases are unable to understand the relationship of inheritance. Hibernate provides a way to map real-time relationships to the database.

Hibernate provides multiple strategies to achieve such a relationship for relational databases. There are three inheritance mapping strategies defined in hibernate:

- Table per class hierarchy
- Table per subclass
- Table per concrete class

Getting ready

In this recipe, we will take a look at table per class hierarchy.

Here, we will create a new data structure that will help you understand the inheritance strategy.

Consider a class, `Employee`. We will extend the `Employee` class into two subclasses—`PermanentEmployee` and `ContractualEmployee`. The following figure represents the relationship:

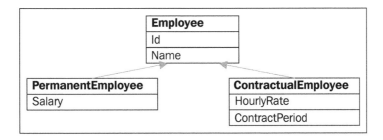

Creating the classes

Update the following code in their respective files:

Source file: `Employee.java`

```
@Entity
@Table(name="employee")
@Inheritance(strategy=InheritanceType.SINGLE_TABLE)
@DiscriminatorColumn(
    name="emp_type"
    , discriminatorType=DiscriminatorType.STRING
    , length=2
)
@DiscriminatorValue(value="E")
public class Employee {

    @Id
    @GeneratedValue
    @Column(name="id")
    private long id;

    @Column(name="name")
    private String name;

    //getters and setters
}
```

Source file: `PermanentEmployee.java`

```
@Entity
@Table(name = "employee")
@DiscriminatorValue(value="PE")
public class PermanentEmployee extends Employee {
```

```
        @Column(name="salary")
        private Double salary;

        //getters and setters
    }
```

Source file: `ContractualEmployee.java`

```
    @Entity
    @Table(name = "employee")
    @DiscriminatorValue(value="CE")
    public class ContractualEmployee extends Employee {

        @Column(name="hourly_rate")
        private Double HourlyRate;

        @Column(name="contract_period")
        private Float ContractPeriod;

        //getters and setters
    }
```

Creating the tables

Use the following table script if the `hibernate.hbm2ddl.auto` configuration property is not set to `create`:

Use the following script to create the `employee` table:

```
    CREATE TABLE `employee` (
      `emp_type` VARCHAR(2) NOT NULL,
      `id` BIGINT(20) NOT NULL AUTO_INCREMENT,
      `name` VARCHAR(255) DEFAULT NULL,
      `contract_period` FLOAT DEFAULT NULL,
      `hourly_rate` DOUBLE DEFAULT NULL,
      `salary` DOUBLE DEFAULT NULL,
      PRIMARY KEY (`id`)
    );
```

Now, hibernate will create a table with the fields of `Employee`, `ContractualEmployee`, `PermanentEmployee`, and one more column defined in the name attribute of the `@DiscriminatorColumn` annotation.

Here, the `Employee` class is the topmost in the hierarchy, and we used some annotation on the `Employee` class. Let's take a look at the annotations used in all three classes.

Annotations used in Employee.java

Following are the annotations used in `Employee.java`:

- ▶ `@Inheritance(strategy=InheritanceType.SINGLE_TABLE)`: This annotation is used to define the inheritance strategy. It is used only on the root class in the hierarchy.

- ▶ `@DiscriminatorColumn(name="emp_type", discriminatorType=DiscriminatorType.STRING, length=2)`: This annotation is used to define the discriminator column for the `SINGLE_TABLE` and `JOINED` mapping strategies. The attributes are as follows:

  - ❑ `name="emp_type"`: hibernate creates a column with the value provided for the name attribute

  - ❑ `discriminatorType=DiscriminatorType.STRING`: This is used to define the datatype of the discriminator column

  - ❑ `length=2`: This is used to define the field size of the discriminator column

- ▶ `@DiscriminatorValue(value="E")`: This annotation defines the value of the discriminator column for this particular class. If the value is not provided, hibernate uses a class name in `DiscriminatorType.STRING`, and the provided specific functions will be used otherwise.

Annotations used in ContractualEmployee.java

Following are the annotations used in `ContractualEmployee.java`:

- ▶ `@DiscriminatorValue(value="CE")`: The value "CE" is used for this particular class

Annotations used in PermanentEmployee.java

Following are the annotations used in `PermanentEmployee.java`:

- ▶ `@DiscriminatorValue(value="PE")`: The value "PE" is used for this particular class

How to do it...

Now, we will save three records of each type of the classes `Employee`, `PermanentEmployee`, and `ContractualEmployee`:

Code

```
Session session = sessionFactory.openSession();

Transaction transaction = session.getTransaction();
```

```
transaction.begin();

Employee employee = new Employee();
employee.setName("Aarush");
session.save(employee);

PermanentEmployee permanentEmployee = new PermanentEmployee();
permanentEmployee.setName("Mike");
permanentEmployee.setSalary(10000D);
session.save(permanentEmployee);

ContractualEmployee contractualEmployee = new ContractualEmployee();
contractualEmployee.setName("Vishal");
contractualEmployee.setHourlyRate(200D);
contractualEmployee.setContractPeriod(100F);
session.save(contractualEmployee);

transaction.commit();

session.close();
```

Output

```
Hibernate: insert into employee (name, emp_type) values (?, 'E')
Hibernate: insert into employee (name, salary, emp_type) values (?,
?, 'PE')
Hibernate: insert into employee (name, contract_period, hourly_rate,
emp_type) values (?, ?, ?, 'CE')
```

The following `employee` table below shows the database table structure after saving three records:

emp_type	id	name	contract_period	hourly_rate	salary
E	1	Aarush	(NULL)	(NULL)	(NULL)
PE	2	Mike	(NULL)	(NULL)	10000
CE	3	Vishal	100	200	(NULL)

How it works...

Here, we defined the `Employee` class as the parent class, and the `ContractualEmployee` and `PermanentEmployee` classes are defined as the subclasses of the `Employee` class.

When we save a record in the parent class, hibernate saves the values in the fields of that particular class and the other columns from the subclasses are saved with a null value.

If we save the record in the `ContractualEmployee` and `PermanentEmployee` subclasses, hibernate saves the values in the fields of the current and parent class.

We can use the value of the `emp_type` column, which is `E` (`Employee`), `PE` is for `PermanentEmployee` and `CE` for `ContractualEmployee` to determine records.

Working with the table per subclass strategy of inheritance

In the previous recipe, we went through the table per class hierarchy inheritance strategy. Table per class hierarchy stores all the rows in a single table and the discriminator column is used to uniquely identify the records. Sometimes, the tables become very large if the hierarchy is deep. In such a case, we can use another strategy called table per subclass.

In the table-per-subclass strategy, hibernate creates separate tables for each class. The relationship exists between the parent and child tables, where the common data is stored in the parent class and the data of the subclass is stored in a separate specific table.

Getting ready

Consider a new table structure as shown in the following table:

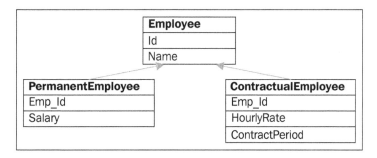

Creating the classes

Update the following code in their respective files:

Source file: `Employee.java`

```
@Entity
@Table(name="employee")
@Inheritance(strategy=InheritanceType.JOINED)
public class Employee {

    @Id
    @GeneratedValue
```

```
    @Column(name="id")
    private long id;

    @Column(name="name")
    private String name;

    // getters and setters
}
```

Source file: `ContractualEmployee.java`

```
@Entity
@Table
@PrimaryKeyJoinColumn(name="emp_id")
public class ContractualEmployee extends Employee {

    @Column(name="hourly_rate")
    private Double HourlyRate;

    @Column(name="contract_period")
    private Float ContractPeriod;

    // getters and setters

}
```

Source file: `PermanentEmployee.java`

```
@Entity
@Table
@PrimaryKeyJoinColumn(name="emp_id")
public class PermanentEmployee extends Employee {

    @Column(name="salary")
    private Double salary;

    // getters and setters

}
```

Creating the tables

Use the following table script if the `hibernate.hbm2ddl.auto` configuration property is not set to `create`:

Use the following script to create the `employee` table:

```
CREATE TABLE `employee` (
    `id` bigint(20) NOT NULL AUTO_INCREMENT,
```

```
  `name` varchar(255) DEFAULT NULL,
  PRIMARY KEY (`id`)
);
```

Use the following script to create the `contractualemployee` table:

```
CREATE TABLE `contractualemployee` (
  `contract_period` float DEFAULT NULL,
  `hourly_rate` double DEFAULT NULL,
  `emp_id` bigint(20) NOT NULL,
  PRIMARY KEY (`emp_id`),
  KEY `FK_EMPLOYEE_ID` (`emp_id`),
  CONSTRAINT `FK_EMPLOYEE_ID`
    FOREIGN KEY (`emp_id`)
    REFERENCES `employee` (`id`)
);
```

Use the following script to create the `permanentemployee` table:

```
CREATE TABLE `permanentemployee` (
  `salary` double DEFAULT NULL,
  `emp_id` bigint(20) NOT NULL,
  PRIMARY KEY (`emp_id`),
  KEY `FK_EMPLOYEE_ID` (`emp_id`),
  CONSTRAINT `_EMPLOYEE_ID`
    FOREIGN KEY (`emp_id`)
    REFERENCES `employee` (`id`)
);
```

In this strategy, we used the `@Inheritance` annotation with `strategy=InheritanceType.JOINED` in the `Employee` parent class only. For the subclasses, we used `@PrimaryKeyJoinColumn(name="emp_id")`. Hibernate will create a foreign key column in all the subtables with the value of the name attribute of the `@PrimaryKeyJoinColumn` annotation.

How to do it...

Now, we will save three records per class for `Employee`, `PermanentEmployee`, and `ContractualEmployee`. Cosider the following code:

Code

```
Session session = sessionFactory.openSession();

Transaction transaction = session.getTransaction();
transaction.begin();
```

```
Employee employee = new Employee();
employee.setName("Aarush");
session.save(employee);

PermanentEmployee permanentEmployee = new PermanentEmployee();
permanentEmployee.setName("Mike");
permanentEmployee.setSalary(10000D);
session.save(permanentEmployee);

ContractualEmployee contractualEmployee = new ContractualEmployee();
contractualEmployee.setName("Vishal");
contractualEmployee.setHourlyRate(200D);
contractualEmployee.setContractPeriod(100F);
session.save(contractualEmployee);

transaction.commit();
session.close();
```

Output

```
Hibernate: insert into employee (name) values (?)
Hibernate: insert into employee (name) values (?)
Hibernate: insert into PermanentEmployee (salary, emp_id) values (?,
?)
Hibernate: insert into employee (name) values (?)
Hibernate: insert into ContractualEmployee (contract_period,
hourly_rate, emp_id) values (?, ?, ?)
```

The following `employee` table shows the database table structure after saving three records:

id	name
1	Aarush
2	Mike
3	Vishal

The following is the database table structure for the `contractualemployee` table:

contract_period	hourly_rate	emp_id
100	200	3

The following is the database table structure for the `permanent employee` table:

salary	emp_id
10000	2

How it works...

Upon careful observation of the data from the three tables and its output, you can understand how this strategy works. In this strategy, the common data is stored in the parent table, which is `Employee` here. The subtable stores the class-specific and common data in the parent table. Also, the subclasses refer to the parent class primary key as a foreign key.

Working with the table per concrete class strategy of inheritance

This is the easiest strategy among all. In this strategy, hibernate creates a different table for each subclass and parent class. The disadvantage of this approach is that duplicate columns are created in the subclass table.

Getting ready

Consider a new table structure as shown in the following table:

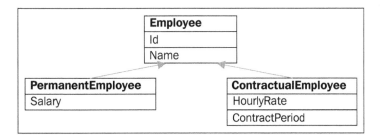

Creating the classes

Update the following code in their respective files:

Source file: `Employee.java`

```
@Entity
@Table(name="employee")
@Inheritance(strategy=InheritanceType.TABLE_PER_CLASS)
public class Employee {

    @Id
```

```
    @GeneratedValue(strategy = GenerationType.TABLE)
    @Column(name="id")
    private long id;

    @Column(name="name")
    private String name;

    //getters and setters
}
```

Source file: `ContractualEmployee.java`

```
@Entity
@AttributeOverrides({
    @AttributeOverride(name="id", column = @Column(name="id")),
    @AttributeOverride(name="name", column = @Column(name="name"))
})
public class ContractualEmployee extends Employee {

    @Column(name="hourly_rate")
    private Double HourlyRate;

    @Column(name="contract_period")
    private Float ContractPeriod;

    //getters and setters
}
```

Source file: `PermanentEmployee.java`

```
@Entity
@AttributeOverrides({
    @AttributeOverride(name="id", column = @Column(name="id")),
    @AttributeOverride(name="name", column = @Column(name="name"))
})
public class PermanentEmployee extends Employee {

    @Column(name="salary")
    private Double salary;

    //getters and setters
}
```

Creating the tables

Use the following table script if the `hibernate.hbm2ddl.auto` configuration property is not set to `create`:

Use the following script to create the `employee` class:

```
CREATE TABLE `employee` (
  `id` bigint(20) NOT NULL,
  `name` varchar(255) DEFAULT NULL,
  PRIMARY KEY (`id`)
);
```

Use the following script to create the `contractualemployee` class:

```
CREATE TABLE `contractualemployee` (
  `id` bigint(20) NOT NULL,
  `name` varchar(255) DEFAULT NULL,
  `contract_period` float DEFAULT NULL,
  `hourly_rate` double DEFAULT NULL,
  PRIMARY KEY (`id`)
);
```

Use the following script to create the `permanentemployee` class:

```
CREATE TABLE `permanentemployee` (
  `id` bigint(20) NOT NULL,
  `name` varchar(255) DEFAULT NULL,
  `salary` double DEFAULT NULL,
  PRIMARY KEY (`id`)
);
```

Annotations used in Employee.java

Following are the annotations used in `Employee.java`:

▸ `@Inheritance(strategy=InheritanceType.TABLE_PER_CLASS)`: This annotation defines the inheritance strategy to be used for an entity class hierarchy. It is used only with the parent or root classes.

Annotations used in PermanentEmployee.java and ContractualEmployee.java

Following are the annotations used in `PermanentEmployee.java` and `ContractualEmployee.java`:

```
@AttributeOverrides({
    @AttributeOverride(name="id", column = @Column(name="id")),
    @AttributeOverride(name="name", column = @Column(name="name"))
})
```

> ▶ `@AttributeOverrides`: This annotation is used to override the mappings of multiple properties or fields

> ▶ `@AttributeOverride`: This annotation is used to override the mappings of basic properties or fields

Hibernate creates a column in the table for the attributes that are overridden by the parent class, in which it generally creates redundant data.

 Note that this strategy does not support the `IDENTITY` and `AUTO` generator strategies; we have to use other generation strategy options or provide a primary key explicitly.

How to do it...

As in the other inheritance strategies, we will insert three records here and see how this strategy works. Update the following code:

Code

```
Session session = sessionFactory.openSession();

Transaction transaction = session.getTransaction();
transaction.begin();

Employee employee = new Employee();
employee.setId(1);
employee.setName("Aarush");
session.save(employee);

PermanentEmployee permanentEmployee = new PermanentEmployee();
permanentEmployee.setId(2);
permanentEmployee.setName("Mike");
permanentEmployee.setSalary(10000D);
session.save(permanentEmployee);
```

```
ContractualEmployee contractualEmployee = new ContractualEmployee();
contractualEmployee.setId(3);
contractualEmployee.setName("Vishal");
contractualEmployee.setHourlyRate(200D);
contractualEmployee.setContractPeriod(100F);
session.save(contractualEmployee);

transaction.commit();

session.close();
```

Output

```
Hibernate: insert into employee (name, id) values (?, ?)
Hibernate: insert into PermanentEmployee (name, salary, id) values (?,
?, ?)
Hibernate: insert into ContractualEmployee (name, contract_period,
hourly_rate, id) values (?, ?, ?, ?)
```

The following `employee` table shows the database table structure after saving three records:

id	name
1	Aarush

The following is the database table structure for the `contractualemployee` table:

id	name	contract_period	hourly_rate
3	Vishal	100	200

The following is the database table structure for the `permanentemployee` table:

id	name	salary
2	Mike	10000

How it works...

Hibernate creates a separate table for all the subclasses. We can see here that an overridden attribute is created in each table.

The disadvantage of this strategy is that if we add, delete, or update a field in the root class, it causes major changes in the subtable as well. This is because in this strategy, the parent class is scattered into the other subclasses and the subclasses use the field of the parent class.

Working with the versioning of objects

Once a record is inserted in the database, we can update it any number of times. The versioning feature of hibernate is useful when we want to know how many times a particular record has been modified. This feature is useful in sensitive applications in the finance domain, where we need to record each and every data movement.

When we use the versioning feature, hibernate inserts the initial version number as zero. Whenever a record is modified, the value of the version is increased by one.

Getting ready

To work with the versioning concept, we have to make a small change in the POJO. We have to create a field with the numeric type and declare this field with the `@version` annotation so that hibernate will consider it to be the versioning column.

Creating the classes

The following code shows the Java file changes for versioning:

Source file: `Employee.java`

```
@Entity
@Table(name = "employee")
public class Employee {

  @Id
  @GeneratedValue
  @Column(name = "id")
  private long id;

  @Column(name = "name")
  private String name;

  @Version
  private long version;

  //getters and setters
}
```

Creating the tables

Use the following table script if the `hibernate.hbm2ddl.auto` configuration property is not set to `create`:

Use the following script to create the `employee` table:

```
CREATE TABLE `employee` (
  `id` bigint(20) NOT NULL AUTO_INCREMENT,
  `name` varchar(255) DEFAULT NULL,
  `version` bigint(20) NOT NULL,
  PRIMARY KEY (`id`)
);
```

How to do it...

Here, we will insert a record and see the table data after a successful insertion. Update the following code:

Code

```
Session session = sessionFactory.openSession();
Transaction transaction = session.getTransaction();
transaction.begin();

Employee employee = new Employee();
employee.setName("Aarush");
session.save(employee);

transaction.commit();
session.close();
```

Output

```
Hibernate: insert into employee (name, version) values (?, ?)
```

The following `employee` table shows a database table structure after saving one record:

id	name	version
1	Aarush	0

How it works...

Hibernate inserts a zero value in the row when a record is created for the first time. This particular value is increased by one on each update operation.

Once you perform an update operation, hibernate updates the version column as well. The following code shows the same:

Code

```
Employee employee = new Employee();
employee.setId(1);
employee.setName("Aaru");
session.saveOrUpdate(employee);
```

Output

```
Hibernate: update employee set name=?, version=? where id=? and
version=?
```

The following `data` table shows the data after an update:

id	name	version
1	Aaru	1

Once we update an employee name here, hibernate increases the version number.

Maintaining the history of an object

In the previous recipe, we used the versioning feature of hibernate to check how many times a particular record has been modified. This is a good feature; however, it gives us just a number. Versioning does not store the modified data anywhere. So, it's hard to find out the previous state of the object before the modification.

As a solution to this, hibernate provides another project called **Envers**.

Envers helps us maintain the history of the database and it keeps track of the modifications in the database table rows. For this to work, we have to change the configuration in the POJO and configuration (`.cfg.xml`) files.

To configure Envers with hibernate, we need JAR files in our project. You can use the following Maven dependency for the Maven-based project:

```
<dependency>
  <groupId>org.hibernate</groupId>
  <artifactId>hibernate-envers</artifactId>
  <version>4.3.10.Final</version>
</dependency>
```

Once we configure Envers in our application, it creates a version table that contains the fields of the original table. Whenever the original table gets modified, hibernate automatically adds an entry in the version table; so, for every insert, update, and delete operation, hibernate inserts the records in the version table. Another table is automatically created by hibernate with the name `revinfo` that stores revision information such as the revision id and revision timestamp.

Getting ready

Here, we will download the required libraries using the Maven dependency. The following code shows how to create the required classes and tables.

Creating the classes

The following code shows an `Employee` POJO and the changes in the configuration file (`*.cgf.xml`):

Source file: `Employee.java`

```
@Entity
@Table(name = "employee")
/* Line 3 */ @Audited
public class Employee {

  @Id
  @GeneratedValue
  private long id;

  @Column(name = "name")
  private String name;

/* Line 13 */  @NotAudited
  @Column(name="password")
  private String password;

  // getters ans setters

}
```

Source file: `hibernate.cfg.xml`

Add the below lines to your configuration file:

```
<listener class="org.hibernate.envers.event.AuditEventListener"
type="post-insert"/>
<listener class="org.hibernate.envers.event.AuditEventListener"
type="post-update"/>
<listener class="org.hibernate.envers.event.AuditEventListener"
type="post-delete"/>
```

Creating the tables

Use the following table script if the `hibernate.hbm2ddl.auto` configuration property is not set to `create`:

Use the following script to create the `employee` table:

```
CREATE TABLE `employee` (
  `id` bigint(20) NOT NULL AUTO_INCREMENT,
  `name` varchar(255) DEFAULT NULL,
  `password` varchar(255) DEFAULT NULL,
  PRIMARY KEY (`id`)
);
```

Use the following script to create the `employee_aud` table:

```
CREATE TABLE `employee_aud` (
  `id` bigint(20) NOT NULL,
  `REV` int(11) NOT NULL,
  `REVTYPE` tinyint(4) DEFAULT NULL,
  `name` varchar(255) DEFAULT NULL,
  PRIMARY KEY (`id`,`REV`),
  KEY `FK_REVISION_ID` (`REV`),
  CONSTRAINT `FK_REVISION_ID` FOREIGN KEY (`REV`) REFERENCES
`revinfo` (`REV`)
);
```

Use the following script to create the `revinfo` table:

```
CREATE TABLE `revinfo` (
  `REV` int(11) NOT NULL AUTO_INCREMENT,
  `REVTSTMP` bigint(20) DEFAULT NULL,
  PRIMARY KEY (`REV`)
);
```

How to do it...

Now, we will insert a record in the `employee` table and take a look at the tables created by hibernate with the data. Update the following code:

Code

```
Session session = sessionFactory.openSession();
Transaction transaction = session.getTransaction();
transaction.begin();

Employee employee = new Employee();
```

```
employee.setName("Aarush");
employee.setPassword("p@$sw0rd");
session.save(employee);

transaction.commit();
session.close();
```

Output

```
/* Line 1 */ Hibernate: insert into employee (name, password) values
(?, ?)
/* Line 2 */ Hibernate: insert into REVINFO (REVTSTMP) values (?)
/* Line 3 */ Hibernate: insert into employee_AUD (REVTYPE, name, id,
REV) values (?, ?, ?, ?)
```

The following employee table shows the data after the insertion is completed:

id	name	password
1	Aarush	p@$sw0rd

The following is the database table structure for the REVINFO table:

REV	REVTSTMP
1	1421832556098

The following is the database table structure for the employee_AUD table:

id	REV	REVTYPE	name
1	1	0	Aarush

How it works...

Now, we will discuss how this feature works. We will take a look at the changes in each file in detail.

Let's consider the Employee.java file. In the Employee class, we added the @Audited annotation at the class level shown in Line 3.

@Audited is present at the class level. This means that hibernate will enable the history of the Employee object and store the changes in the revision table.

Another useful annotation used in this class is @NotAudited, which is shown in Line 13.

Using the `@Audited` annotation at the class level means that all the fields of that class are involved in the auditing process. If we do not want any field to be involved in the auditing process, the `@NotAudited` annotation is used. For instance, here we annotate a password field with the `@NotAudited` annotation, so hibernate will ignore this field during auditing.

Now, let's consider the `hibernate.cfg.xml` file. In this configuration file, we added three new listener tags, where the class attribute defines the `Listener` class and the type attribute defines a type of operation, such as `post-insert`, `post-update`, and `post-delete`.

There are many events available in hibernate. Here, `post-insert` means that the auditing is done after the insertion is completed. This works in a similar way for `post-update` and `post-delete`.

There's more...

Once we execute the code, hibernate will create three tables:

- ▶ `employee`: This represents the `Employee` class.
- ▶ `employee_AUD`: This represents the audit table for the `Employee` class. Hibernate will create an audit table by the concatenation of the actual table name as a prefix and the "`_AUD`" value as a suffix if value is not provided.
- ▶ `revinfo`: This stores the revision information, such as the revision id and revision timestamp.

We can change the suffix and prefix value of the table as well as the audit table name in the following way:

```
@AuditTable(value="emp_history")
public class Employee {
  // other fields and setters/getters
}
```

Now, hibernate will create the table name, `emp_history`; the prefix and suffix are ignored in this case.

Changing the suffix by changing the property in the configuration file

To change the audit table suffix, you can update the following configurations:

```
<property name="org.hibernate.envers.auditTableSuffix">
  _history
</property>
```

You can also use:

```
<property name="org.hibernate.envers.audit_table_suffix">
  _history
</property>
```

 Hibernate uses _history as the suffix if not provided.
The _AUD" suffix is used by default.

Changing the prefix by changing the property in the configuration file

To change the audit table prefix, you can update the following configurations:

```
<property name="org.hibernate.envers.auditTablePrefix">
  history_
</property>
```

You can also use:

```
<property name="org.hibernate.envers.audit_table_prefix">
  history_
</property>
```

 Hibernate uses history_ as the prefix if not provided.
The "" prefix is used by default.

Now, hibernate will create an audit table with the given configuration, which will contain all auditable fields and the REV and REVTYPE column.

The REV and REVTYPE columns are used to maintain the revisions. To change the name of the REV and REVTYPE columns, use the following code:

Renaming the REV column

To change the revision field name, you can update the following configurations:

```
<property name="org.hibernate.envers.revision_field_name">
  REV_COL
</property>
```

You can also use:

```
<property name="org.hibernate.envers.revisionFieldName">
  REV_COL
</property>
```

Hibernate uses `REV_COL` as the column name; if not provided, `REV` is used by default.

Renaming the REVTYPE column

To change the revision type field name, you can update the following configurations:

```
<property name="org.hibernate.envers.revision_type_field_name">
  REVTYPE_COL
</property>
```

You can also use:

```
<property name="org.hibernate.envers.revisionTypeFieldName">
  REVTYPE_COL
</property>
```

 Hibernate uses `REVTYPE_COL` as the column name; if not provided, `REVTYPE` is used by default.

Working with an interceptor

As we know, in the hibernate persistent lifecycle, a particular object travels from state to state, from transient, persistent, to detached. During processing, it may commit or roll back before it reaches the last state. Sometimes, we need to perform some additional tasks such as cleanup, log or some operations on the object between different states of the persistent life cycle. To perform such activities, hibernate provides a useful and pluggable feature called **interceptor**.

Interceptor, as the name suggests, is used to intercept any operation. Interceptors apply hooks inside the logic. In hibernate, we have some built-in interceptors that help us intercept our logic.

Generally, an interceptor is used to log monitor data that is input and to validate it. You can also change or overwrite it at runtime. Let's take a look at the next example.

Getting ready

In this recipe, we will discuss the use of a basic interceptor and some methods of intercepting. Here, we will try to save the `employee` object and capturing the log while saving an object.

Creating the classes

For this recipe, we will create an `Employee` class:

Source file: `Employee.java`

```
@Entity
@Table(name = "employee")
public class Employee {

  @Id
  @GeneratedValue
  private long id;

  @Column(name = "name")
  private String name;

  // getters ans setters
}
```

Creating the tables

Use the following table script if the `hibernate.hbm2ddl.auto` configuration property is not set to `create`:

Use the following script to create the `employee` table:

```
CREATE TABLE `employee` (
  `id` bigint(20) NOT NULL AUTO_INCREMENT,
  `name` varchar(255) DEFAULT NULL,
  PRIMARY KEY (`id`)
);
```

How to do it...

First of all, we need to create an interceptor class that extends `EmptyInterceptor`, which implements the `org.hibernate.Interceptor` interface. Update the following code:

Code

Source file: `CustomInterceptor.java`

```
import org.hibernate.EmptyInterceptor;
import org.hibernate.type.Type;
public class CustomInterceptor extends EmptyInterceptor {

  /* Line 3 */ public boolean onSave(Object entity, Serializable id,
  Object[] state, String[] propertyNames, Type[] types) {
    System.out.println("On Save");
    System.out.println("entity: " + entity);
```

```
        System.out.println("id: " + id);
        System.out.println("state: " + Arrays.toString(state));
        System.out.println("propertyNames: " +
    Arrays.toString(propertyNames));
        System.out.println("types: " + Arrays.toString(types));
        return false;
      }

    /* Line 13 */ public void preFlush(Iterator iterator) {
        System.out.println("\n\nPre flush");
        while (iterator.hasNext()) {
          System.out.println(iterator.next());
        }
      }

    /* Line 20 */ public void postFlush(Iterator iterator) {
        System.out.println("\n\nPost flush");
        while (iterator.hasNext()) {
          System.out.println(iterator.next());
        }
      }
    }
```

Source file: `InterceptorTest.java`

```
/* Line 1 */ CustomInterceptor interceptor = new CustomInterceptor();
/* Line 2 */ Session session =
sessionFactory.withOptions().interceptor(interceptor).openSession(
);
/* Line 3 */ Transaction tx = null;
/* Line 4 */ tx = session.beginTransaction();

/* Line 6 */ Employee employee = new Employee();
/* Line 7 */ employee.setName("Vishal");
/* Line 8 */ session.saveOrUpdate(employee);

/* Line 9 */ tx.commit();
/* Line 10 */ session.close();
/* Line 11 */ sessionFactoy.close();
```

Output:

```
On Save
entity: Employee:
  Id: 0
  Name: Vishal
```

```
id: null
state: [Vishal]
propertyNames: [name]
types: [org.hibernate.type.StringType@4abd7e7c]
Hibernate: insert into employee (name) values (?)


Pre flush
Employee:
  Id: 1
  Name: Vishal


Post flush
Employee:
  Id: 1
  Name: Vishal
```

How it works...

In the previous section, we created two different Java source files. the first one is CustomInterceptor.java, which overrides some methods of the EmptyInterceptor superclass, and the other is the InterceptorTest.java executable class, which shows the code to test the mechanism.

Now, we will consider the code in detail.

The working of InterceptorTest.java

This is an executable class and contains the main method.

In Line 1, we created the object of the CustomInterceptor class.

Line 2 shows how to provide options to SessionFactory on runtime; builder design patterns are used to provide the interceptor to the session. The withOptions() method returns the instance of SessionBuilder. On top of it, we set an interceptor that is an instance of CustomInterceptor using the interceptor() method and then opened a new session.

The code from Line 3 onward creates an employee object and saves it within the boundary of the transaction.

The working of CustomInterceptor.java

Here, we extended the EmptyInterceptor class and implemented the three methods.

The working of onSave Method

The `onSave` method is called before the object is saved to the database. Constructor of `onSave` is shown in the following code:

```
boolean onSave(Object entity,
               Serializable id,
               Object[] state,
               String[] propertyNames,
               Type[] types)
               throws CallbackException
```

The arguments passed are as follows:

- ▶ **Object entity**: This shows the requested object for save. Here, the employee is passed, so it shows the details of the employee. One important thing shown here is that the object is not saved while processing this method, so the `id` fields are set to `0`.

- ▶ **Serializable id**: This shows the serializable id. Here, it is `null` because we are saving the object.

- ▶ **Object[] state**: This contains the values to be saved; here, `vishal`, as we have only one field in the POJO.

- ▶ **String[] propertyNames**: This contains the property name with respect to the `state` field; here, the `name` field, where the value of this field is stored in the `state` object.

- ▶ **Type[] types**: This field contains the datatype of all the fields that are sent to save.

The working of preFlush Method

Another of the methods we implemented is `preFlush`. This method is called after commit is completed and just before flush is started. Use of `preFlush()` is shown in the following code:

```
/* Line 13 */ public void preFlush(Iterator iterator) {
  System.out.println("\n\nPre flush");
  while (iterator.hasNext()) {
    System.out.println(iterator.next());
  }
}
```

In the output, you will find `id=1`, which was `0` in the `onSave()` method, because the object is saved to the database. The argument iterator returns the object whose id is going to be flushed out.

The working of postFlush Method

The last of the three methods is `postFlush`. This method is called after commit is completed and just before flush is completed. Use of `postFlush()` is shown in the following code:

```
/* Line 20 */ public void postFlush(Iterator iterator) {
  System.out.println("\n\nPost flush");
  while (iterator.hasNext()) {
```

```
        System.out.println(iterator.next());
    }
}
```

Working with batch processing

Sometimes, we need to save a large number of records in the database. Let's say we need 10,000 records in the database, and we use the basic approach to save the records. The way to do this is as follows:

```
Session session = SessionFactory.openSession();
Transaction tx = session.beginTransaction();
for ( int i=0; i<100000; i++ ) {
    Employee employee = new Employee(.....);
    session.save(employee);
}
tx.commit();
session.close();
```

Two known issues in the preceding method are as follows:

 ▸ Hibernate will try to save each object to the database one by one; this will be time consuming and may increase the load on the database and application as well

 ▸ The application may face OutOfMemoryException because hibernate saves all the new employee objects in the second-level cache

To overcome these problems and to make the application faster, we need to use batch processing. Hibernate supports batch processing, which is the same as a JDBC batch processing.

Getting ready

The following codes help you to create the required classes and tables for this recipe.

Creating the classes

To perform batch processing using hibernate, we need to create the Employee class and make a little change in configuration file; here, we need to make the changes in hibernate. cfg.xml. Update the following code:

Source file: Employee.java

```
@Entity
@Table(name = "employee")
public class Employee {
```

```
@Id
@GeneratedValue
private long id;

@Column(name = "name")
private String name;

// getters and setters
}
```

Source file: `hibernate.cfg.xml`

```
...
  <property name="hibernate.jdbc.batch_size">
     50
</property>
  <property name="hibernate.cache.use_second_level_cache">
false
</property>
  ...
```

How to do it...

First of all, we will take a look at an executable code snippet that shows how to use batch processing in hibernate:

Source file: `BatchProcessingMain.java`

```
Session session = sessionFactory.openSession();
Transaction transaction = session.beginTransaction();
for (int i = 0; i < 10000; i++) {
  Employee employee = new Employee();
  employee.setName("Name : " + String.valueOf(i));
  session.save(employee);
/* Line 7 */  if (i % 50 == 0) {
/* Line 8 */    session.flush();
/* Line 9*/    session.clear();
  }
}
transaction.commit();
session.close();
```

The following is the output for the preceding code:

```
Hibernate: insert into employee (name) values (?)
Hibernate: insert into employee (name) values (?)
Hibernate: insert into employee (name) values (?)
.
.
.
Hibernate: insert into employee (name) values (?)
```

How it works...

First of all, the change in `hibernate.cfg.xml` is `hibernate.jdbc.batch_size = 50`, informing hibernate to create a batch of `50` for the batch operation. Another is `hibernate.cache.use_second_level_cache = false`, informing hibernate not to cache the object as we were doing a batch operation, and it is unnecessary to store the objects in the cache.

In the executable code, we looped 10,000 times and saved the records using the `session.save(...)` method. In `Line 7`, we checked whether the value of the `i` variable was equal to a multiple of `50` and then flushed and cleared the session.

The `Session.flush()` method was used to persist a record and sent to the database. You cannot actually see it from the database or using another session/thread because this record is not committed yet. Once a transaction is committed, the records are available for the other session/thread.

The `Session.clear()` method clears all the cached records from the session and releases the memory.

8
Integration with Other Frameworks

In this chapter, we will cover the following recipes:

- ▶ Integration with Spring
- ▶ Integration with Struts

Introduction

In the today's world, many frameworks are available to make the development process easier. A framework typically provides an architecture that is best suited for industry development, and it also provides the flexibility to integrate one framework with another. Hence, the demand for this type of framework has increased.

Hibernate provides easy integration with frameworks such as Spring and Struts. In this chapter, we will take a look at how to integrate hibernate ORM with Spring version 4 and Struts version 2.

Integration with Spring

Spring is an open source development framework that helps developers make the development process much better. Spring is known for **DI (dependency injection)**, **IoC (inversion of control)**, **AOP (aspects-oriented programming)**, core and test container, data access/integration with JDBC, ORM, **JMS(Java Messaging Service)**, web integration with servlet, portlet, and other frameworks, such as Struts, and Spring **DAO (data access object)** support. We can use the Spring framework in either a Java Standalone application or a JEE enterprise application.

The official site for Spring is `https://spring.io`, which gives detailed information about all the projects by Spring, and `http://projects.spring.io/spring-framework/`, which is for the Spring framework.

In this recipe, we will take a look at how to integrate hibernate with Spring using a Spring DAO pattern. Also, we will assume that you have a basic knowledge of patterns, Maven, and Spring core.

Getting ready

Before moving forward, let's understand DAO.

DAO stands for data access object. It is a pattern that provides an abstract interface layer to access the database or a persistent layer using some predefined methods.

Generally, we have two different styles of DAO.

> **Generic DAO or DAO per application**: This is a central DAO that provides all the methods for a CRUD operation, such as `Save`, `Delete`, `Update`, `Get by id`, and so on. This type of DAO is useful when we have to perform a common operation across the application.

> **DAO per class**: In this style, we have a separate DAO for each class. It also contains generic methods such as `Save`, `Delete`, `Update`, and `Get by id`, and it may have its own methods as well.

In this example, we will use the DAO per class method.

The project dependencies

Here, we will create a Maven project, so all project dependencies mentioned will be in `pom.xml`:

Source file: `pom.xml`

```
<project xmlns="http://maven.apache.org/POM/4.0.0" xmlns:xsi="http://
www.w3.org/2001/XMLSchema-instance"
  xsi:schemaLocation="http://maven.apache.org/POM/4.0.0
  http://maven.apache.org/maven-v4_0_0.xsd">
  <modelVersion>4.0.0</modelVersion>
  <groupId>com.packt</groupId>
  <artifactId>SpringHibernateExample</artifactId>
  <packaging>war</packaging>
  <version>0.0.1-SNAPSHOT</version>
  <name>SpringHiber Maven Webapp</name>
  <url>http://maven.apache.org</url>
  <properties>
```

```
      <spring-framework.version>4.0.3.RELEASE</spring-
      framework.version>
      <hibernate.version>4.3.5.Final</hibernate.version>
   </properties>

   <dependencies>
     <dependency>
       <groupId>org.springframework</groupId>
       <artifactId>spring-context</artifactId>
       <version>${spring-framework.version}</version>
     </dependency>
     <dependency>
       <groupId>org.springframework</groupId>
       <artifactId>spring-tx</artifactId>
       <version>${spring-framework.version}</version>
     </dependency>

     <dependency>
       <groupId>org.springframework</groupId>
       <artifactId>spring-orm</artifactId>
       <version>${spring-framework.version}</version>
     </dependency>

     <dependency>
       <groupId>org.hibernate</groupId>
       <artifactId>hibernate-core</artifactId>
       <version>${hibernate.version}</version>
     </dependency>

     <dependency>
       <groupId>mysql</groupId>
       <artifactId>mysql-connector-java</artifactId>
       <version>5.1.9</version>
     </dependency>

   </dependencies>
   <build>
     <finalName>SpringHibernateExample</finalName>
   </build>
</project>
```

Here, we used only the required dependency for this recipe.

Creating the tables

Use the following script to create the tables if you are not using `hbm2dll=create|update`:

Table: `film`

```
create table film (
    id bigint not null auto_increment,
    name varchar(255),
    releaseYear bigint,
    primary key (id)
);
```

Creating a model class

A model class is the same as a POJO. Execute the following code:

Source file: `Film.java`

```java
package com.packt.modal;

import javax.persistence.Column;
import javax.persistence.Entity;
import javax.persistence.GeneratedValue;
import javax.persistence.GenerationType;
import javax.persistence.Id;
import javax.persistence.Table;

@Entity
@Table(name = "film")
public class Film {


  public Film() {

  }

  public Film(String name, long releaseYear) {
    super();
    this.name = name;
    this.releaseYear = releaseYear;
  }

  @Id
  @GeneratedValue(strategy = GenerationType.IDENTITY)
  private long id;
```

```
@Column
private String name;

@Column
private long releaseYear;

public long getId() {
  return id;
}

public void setId(long id) {
  this.id = id;
}

public String getName() {
  return name;
}

public void setName(String name) {
  this.name = name;
}

public long getReleaseYear() {
  return releaseYear;
}

public void setReleaseYear(long releaseYear) {
  this.releaseYear = releaseYear;
}

@Override
public String toString() {
  return "Film [id=" + id + ", name=" + name + ", releaseYear="
      + releaseYear + "]";
}

}
```

Creating an interface – DAO

Here, we will create an interface for the film class by adding the following code:

Source file: FilmDao.java

```
package com.packt.dao;

import java.util.List;
```

```
import com.packt.modal.Film;

public interface FilmDao {

  public void save(Film film);

  public List<Film> getAll();

  public Film getById(long filmId);
}
```

The Spring configuration

Spring is known for dependency injection, where it allows the user to inject a dependency from a hard code and has the facility to provide the configuration via XML. Here, we will create `spring.xml` in which we will write all the beans that are used at runtime:

Source file: `spring.xml`

```xml
<?xml version="1.0" encoding="UTF-8"?>
<beans xmlns="http://www.springframework.org/schema/beans"
  xmlns:xsi="http://www.w3.org/2001/XMLSchema-instance"
  xmlns:tx="http://www.springframework.org/schema/tx"
  xsi:schemaLocation="http://www.springframework.org/schema/beans
    http://www.springframework.org/schema/beans/spring-beans.xsd
    http://www.springframework.org/schema/tx
    http://www.springframework.org/schema/tx/spring-tx-4.0.xsd">

  <!-- Line 3 --> <bean id="dataSource"
  class="org.springframework.jdbc.datasource.
DriverManagerDataSource">
    <!-- Line 4 --> <property name="driverClassName"
    value="com.mysql.jdbc.Driver" />
    <!-- Line 5  --> <property name="url"
    value="jdbc:mysql://localhost:3306/springHibernateIntegration"
/>
    <!-- Line 6  --> <property name="username" value="root" />
    <!-- Line 7  --> <property name="password" value="root" />
  </bean>

  <!-- Line 9  --> <bean id="hibernate4AnnotatedSessionFactory"
    class="org.springframework.orm.
    hibernate4.LocalSessionFactoryBean">
    <!-- Line 10  --> <property name="dataSource" ref="dataSource"
/>
    <!-- Line 11  --> <property name="annotatedClasses">
```

```
            <list>
              <!-- Line 13   --> <value>com.packt.modal.Film</value>
            </list>
          </property>
          /* Line 16 */ <property name="hibernateProperties">
            <props>
              /* Line 18 */ <prop key="hibernate.dialect">
      org.hibernate.dialect.MySQLDialect
      </prop>
              <prop
      key="hibernate.current_session_context_class">thread</prop>
              <prop key="hibernate.format_sql">true</prop>
              <prop key="hibernate.hbm2ddl.auto">create</prop>
            </props>
          </property>
        </bean>

        /* Line 26 */ <bean id="filmDao"
        class="com.packt.dao.FilmDaoImpl">
          /* Line 27 */ <property name="sessionFactory"
          ref="hibernate4AnnotatedSessionFactory" />
        </bean>
      </beans>
```

Here, `Line 3` creates a bean with id, `dataSource`, which means that it creates an instance of the `org.springframework.jdbc.datasource.DriverManagerDataSource` class, which is mentioned in the class attribute of the bean.

The properties are shown in `Lines 4, 5, 6,` and 7, which are `driverClassName`, `url`, `username`, and `password` respectively. They are fields declared in the `org.springframework.jdbc.datasource.DriverManagerDataSource` class and are used to provide the database-related configuration.

The code shown in `Lines 4, 5, 6,` and 7 uses a setter-based injection to inject the value in to the bean.

The bean declared in `Line 9` is used to create the object of `SessionFactory`, which we created using the `hibernate.cfg.xml` file in the core hibernate application.

The code written in `Line 10` provides a reference to the `dataSource` bean to use the database property.

The code written in `Line 13` shows the classes used in the application, so it will be scanned at the start of the application.

The code written in `Line 16` is used to provide a hibernate-specific property to `SessionFactory`.

Line 26 shows the initialization of `FilmDaoImpl`, and Line 27 injects the object of `SessionFactory` into the `FilmDaoImpl` class. So, we can use it directly without creating an object of that class using a new keyword as Spring will create an instance of the particular class for us.

Reviewing the project structure

After creating those files, look into your Maven project structure, which is created with Eclipse, as shown in the following screenshot:

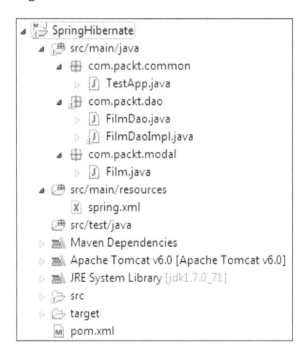

How to do it...

In this section, we will discuss the implementation of the `FilmDao` interface and `main` class to run our code using the `main` method.

The DAO implementations

This shows the implementation of the `FilmDao.java` interface:

Code

Source File: `FilmDaoImpl.java`

```
package com.packt.dao;
```

```
import java.util.List;

import org.hibernate.Criteria;
import org.hibernate.Session;
import org.hibernate.SessionFactory;
import org.hibernate.Transaction;
import org.hibernate.criterion.Restrictions;

import com.packt.modal.Film;

public class FilmDaoImpl implements FilmDao {

  SessionFactory sessionFactory;

  /* Line 17 */ public void setSessionFactory(SessionFactory
  sessionFactory) {
    this.sessionFactory = sessionFactory;
  }

  /* Line 21 */ public void save(Film film) {
    Session session = this.sessionFactory.openSession();
    Transaction tx = session.beginTransaction();
    session.saveOrUpdate(film);
    tx.commit();
    session.close();
  }

  /* Line 29 */ public List<Film> getAll() {
    Session session = this.sessionFactory.openSession();
    List<Film> filmList = session.createQuery("from Film").list();
    session.close();
    return filmList;
  }

  /* Line 36 */ public Film getById(long filmId) {
    Session session = this.sessionFactory.openSession();
    Criteria criteria = session.createCriteria(Film.class);
    criteria.add(Restrictions.eq("id", filmId));
    Film film = (Film) criteria.uniqueResult();
    session.close();
    return film;
  }

}
```

The `FileDaoImpl` class implements the `FileDao` interface; so, it shows the implementation for all the methods defined in the interface.

The setter written in `Line 17` is used to inject `SessionFactory` in this class. Also, `Line 21` shows the implementation of the `save()` method, `Line 29` shows the implementation of the `getAll()` method, and `Line 36` shows the implementation of the `getById()` method.

Now, the following code shows an executable class that is used to test all the functionalities:

Source file: `TestApp.java`

```
package com.packt.common;

import java.util.List;
import org.springframework.context.support.
ClassPathXmlApplicationContext
;
import com.packt.dao.FilmDao;
import com.packt.modal.Film;

public class TestApp {

  public static void main(String[] args) {

    /* Line 14 */ClassPathXmlApplicationContext context = new
    ClassPathXmlApplicationContext("spring.xml");

    /* Line 16 */FilmDao filmDao = (FilmDao)
    context.getBean("filmDao");

    /* Line 18 */Film film1 = new Film("Film 1", 2013);
    /* Line 19 */filmDao.save(film1);
    /* Line 20 */System.out.println("Film Saved: " + film1);

    /* Line 22 */Film film2 = new Film("Film 2", 2014);
    /* Line 23 */filmDao.save(film2);
    /* Line 24 */System.out.println("Film Saved: " + film2);

    /* Line 26 */System.out.println("\nAll Film List");
    /* Line 27 */List<Film> films = filmDao.getAll();
    /* Line 28 */for (Film filmObj : films) {
    /* Line 29 */  System.out.println(filmObj);
    /* Line 30 */}

    /* Line 32 */System.out.println("\nGet Film by id 1");
    /* Line 33 */Film film = filmDao.getById(1);
```

```
        /* Line 34 */System.out.println(film);
        /* Line 35 */context.close();
    }
}
```

Output

The output will be as follows:

```
Hibernate: drop table if exists film
Hibernate: create table film (id bigint not null auto_increment,
name varchar(255), releaseYear bigint, primary key (id))

Hibernate: insert into film (name, releaseYear) values (?, ?)
Film Saved: Film [id=1, name=Film 1, releaseYear=2013]
Hibernate: insert into film (name, releaseYear) values (?, ?)
Film Saved: Film [id=2, name=Film 2, releaseYear=2014]

All Film List
Hibernate: select film0_.id as id1_0_, film0_.name as name2_0_,
film0_.releaseYear as releaseY3_0_ from film film0_
Film [id=1, name=Film 1, releaseYear=2013]
Film [id=2, name=Film 2, releaseYear=2014]

Get Film by id 1
Hibernate: select this_.id as id1_0_0_, this_.name as name2_0_0_,
this_.releaseYear as releaseY3_0_0_ from film this_ where
this_.id=?
Film [id=1, name=Film 1, releaseYear=2013]
```

How it works...

Let's consider the code line by line to understand it.

In the line, `/* Line 14 */ClassPathXmlApplicationContext context = new ClassPathXmlApplicationContext("spring.xml");`, we created an instance of the `ClassPathXmlApplicationContext` class and provided our bean configuration file, `spring.xml`, as a constructor argument. As we used the `ClassPathXmlApplicationContext` class, hibernate will look in the classpath for `spring.xml` and load all the beans defined in this file.

Using the line, `/* Line 16 */FilmDao filmDao = (FilmDao) context.getBean("filmDao");`, we fetched a bean from the context with id `filmDao`. It will return an instance of the `FilmDaoImpl` class. The bean is declared in the `spring.xml` file in Line 26: `<bean id="filmDao" class="com.packt.dao.FilmDaoImpl">`.

Lines `18` to `24` are used to create a different instance of `Film` and save it to the database using the DAO method, `save(Film film);`.

Lines `26` to `30` are used to get all the films using the `getAll();` method.

Lines `32` to `35` are used to get `Film` by `id` using the `getById(long filmId);` method.

Integration with Struts

Struts is an open source web application framework that is designed to support the development life cycle, which includes building, deploying, and maintaining the application. Struts is based on the **MVC** (**Model View Controller**) pattern. It is available under Apache License.

The official site of Struts to download the distribution, support, contribution, and tutorials is `https://struts.apache.org/`.

Here, we will create a Maven-based Struts web application to understand how to integrate hibernate with Struts. In this recipe, we will continue to use the DAO pattern.

Struts has no plugin available for integration with hibernate, so we will manage all hibernate code manually.

Getting ready

In this section, we will create a code file required for hibernate and Struts with a detailed description.

The project dependencies

Here, we will create a Maven project; so, all project dependencies will be mentioned in `pom.xml`:

Source file: `pom.xml`

```
<project xmlns="http://maven.apache.org/POM/4.0.0"
xmlns:xsi="http://www.w3.org/2001/XMLSchema-instance"
  xsi:schemaLocation="http://maven.apache.org/POM/4.0.0
http://maven.apache.org/maven-v4_0_0.xsd">
  <modelVersion>4.0.0</modelVersion>
  <groupId>com.packt</groupId>
  <artifactId>StrutsHibernate</artifactId>
  <packaging>war</packaging>
  <version>0.0.1-SNAPSHOT</version>
  <name>StrutsHibernate Maven Webapp</name>
  <url>http://maven.apache.org</url>

  <properties>
```

```
    <struts2-core.version>2.3.24</struts2-core.version>
    <hibernate.version>4.3.5.Final</hibernate.version>
</properties>

<dependencies>
  <dependency>
    <groupId>org.apache.struts</groupId>
    <artifactId>struts2-core</artifactId>
    <version>${struts2-core.version}</version>
  </dependency>

  <dependency>
    <groupId>org.hibernate</groupId>
    <artifactId>hibernate-core</artifactId>
    <version>${hibernate.version}</version>
  </dependency>

  <dependency>
    <groupId>mysql</groupId>
    <artifactId>mysql-connector-java</artifactId>
    <version>5.1.9</version>
  </dependency>
</dependencies>
<build>
  <finalName>StrutsHibernate</finalName>
</build>
</project>
```

In this pom file, we covered the required dependency for the Struts core, hibernate, and the MySQL connector only.

The hibernate configuration

We will create a hibernate configuration file to provide the database configuration:

Source file: `hibernate.cfg.xml`

```
<?xml version='1.0' encoding='UTF-8'?>
<!DOCTYPE hibernate-configuration PUBLIC
    "-//Hibernate/Hibernate Configuration DTD 3.0//EN"
    "http://www.hibernate.org/dtd/hibernate-configuration-3.0.dtd">
<hibernate-configuration>
  <session-factory>
    <property
name="hibernate.dialect">org.hibernate.dialect.MySQLDialect</prope
rty>
```

```
    <property
name="hibernate.connection.url">jdbc:mysql://localhost:3306/Struts
HibernateIntegration</property>
        <property name="hibernate.connection.username">root</property>
        <property name="hibernate.connection.password">root</property>
        <property name="show_sql">true</property>
        <property name="hbm2ddl.auto">create</property>

        <mapping class="com.packt.modal.Film" />
    </session-factory>
</hibernate-configuration>
```

Creating the tables

Use the following script to create the tables if you are not using `hbm2dll=create|update`:

Table: `film`

```
    create table film (
        id bigint not null auto_increment,
        name varchar(255),
        releaseYear bigint,
        primary key (id)
    );
```

Creating a model class

A model class is the same as a POJO. Here, we will use the same POJO class that was created in the previous recipe, *Integration with Spring*. Also, we will use the `Film.java` file from the previous recipe.

Creating an interface – DAO

Here, we will create an interface for the film class. Execute the following code:

Source file: `FilmDao.java`

```
package com.packt.dao;

import java.util.List;

import com.packt.modal.Film;

public interface FilmDao {

  public void save(Film film);

  public List<Film> getAll();
}
```

The Struts configuration

We need to add a filter in web.xml, create Action, and also map Actions with the view part.

The deployment descriptor

As this is a web-based example, we need to register the Struts filter in web.xml so that every web request coming from the user passes through that filter only:

Source file: web.xml

```
<!DOCTYPE web-app PUBLIC
  "-//Sun Microsystems, Inc.//DTD Web Application 2.3//EN"
  "http://java.sun.com/dtd/web-app_2_3.dtd" >

<web-app>
  <display-name>Struts Hibernate Web Application</display-name>

  <filter>
    <filter-name>struts2</filter-name>
    <filter-class>
    org.apache.struts2.dispatcher.ng.filter.StrutsPrepareAndExecuteFil
ter
    </filter-class>
  </filter>

  <filter-mapping>
    <filter-name>struts2</filter-name>
    <url-pattern>/*</url-pattern>
  </filter-mapping>

</web-app>
```

In this file, the filter is added with url-pattern /*, and org.apache.struts2. dispatcher.ng.filter.StrutsPrepareAndExecuteFilter is added as the filter class so that every request is passed through the StrutsPrepareAndExecuteFilter filter.

Creating an Action class

In this class, we create the actions that are used to perform operations:

Source file: FileAction.java

```
package com.packt.action;

import java.util.ArrayList;
import java.util.List;
```

```
import org.hibernate.SessionFactory;

import com.opensymphony.xwork2.ActionSupport;
import com.opensymphony.xwork2.ModelDriven;
import com.packt.common.HibernateUtil;
import com.packt.dao.FilmDao;
import com.packt.dao.FilmDaoImpl;
import com.packt.modal.Film;

/* Line 15 */ public class FilmAction extends ActionSupport
implements ModelDriven {

  Film film = new Film();
  List<Film> films = new ArrayList<Film>();

  @Override
  /* Line 21 */ public String execute() throws Exception {
  /* Line 22 */    return SUCCESS;
  }

  public List<Film> getFilms() {
    return films;
  }

  public void setFilms(List<Film> films) {
    this.films = films;
  }

  public Object getModel() {
    return film;
  }

  /* Line 37 */ public String saveFilm(){
    SessionFactory sessionFactory =
HibernateUtil.getSessionFactory();
    FilmDao filmDao = new FilmDaoImpl(sessionFactory);
    filmDao.save(film);

    // refresh films
    films = filmDao.getAll();

    return SUCCESS;
  }
```

```
/* Line 48 */ public String listAllFilms(){
    films = null;
    SessionFactory sessionFactory =
HibernateUtil.getSessionFactory();

    FilmDao filmDao = new FilmDaoImpl(sessionFactory);
    films = filmDao.getAll();

    return SUCCESS;
}

}
```

In Line 15, you can find the extends ActionSupport class. The ActionSupport implements multiple interfaces, including the Action interface.

Consider the following code:

```
public interface Action {
    public static final String SUCCESS = "success";
    public static final String NONE = "none";
    public static final String ERROR = "error";
    public static final String INPUT = "input";
    public static final String LOGIN = "login";
    public String execute() throws Exception;
}
```

Here, we override the execute() method which returns SUCCESS as a result. SUCCESS is the final variable of the Action interface, which provides the result name and is used in the struts.xml mapping file to redirect if it is success.

Also, Line 15 shows the implements ModelDriven interface, which is used to convert the form data into an object automatically.

The Struts Action mapping

Add the following code:

Source file: struts.xml

```
<?xml version="1.0" encoding="UTF-8" ?>
<!DOCTYPE struts PUBLIC "-//Apache Software Foundation//DTD Struts
Configuration 2.0//EN" "http://struts.apache.org/dtds/struts-
2.0.dtd">

<struts>
    /* Line 5 */ <constant name="struts.devMode" value="true" />
```

```
    <package name="default" namespace="/" extends="struts-default">

    /* Line 9 */ <action name="addFilmAction"
class="com.packt.action.FilmAction" method="saveFilm">
        /* Line 10 */ <result name="success">view/film.jsp</result>
    </action>

    /* Line 13 */ <action name="listFilmAction"
class="com.packt.action.FilmAction" method="listAllFilms">
        /* Line 14 */ <result name="success">view/film.jsp</result>
    </action>

    </package>
</struts>
```

This file shows the handler for all requests and decides the proper responses accordingly.

`Line 5` sets the `struts.devMode` constant to `true`; Struts will consider the current environment to be the development environment and provide more information and logs on the console or output window. This option is not preferred in the production environment.

`Line 9` creates an action with the name `"addFilmAction"`, the `com.packt.action.FilmAction` class, and the method is `saveFilm`. It means that if a request comes for the `addFilmAction` action, it will execute the `saveFilm` method of the `com.packt.action.FilmAction` class. If the `saveFilm` method returns success as an output, it will return `film.jsp` as the response written in `Line 10`.

`Lines 13` and `14` are used to create the action for the list of all `Films`.

Reviewing the project structure

After creating these many files, look into your Maven project structure, which is created with Eclipse, as shown in the following screenshot:

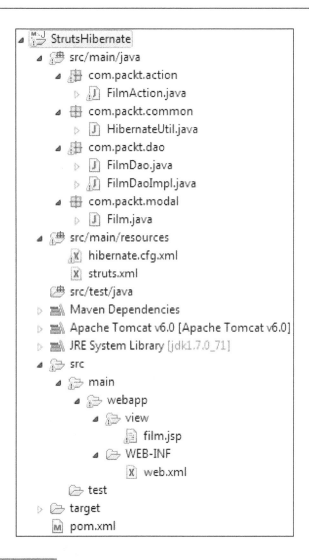

How to do it...

In this section, we will discuss the implementation of the FilmDao interface and create a .jsp file, which is used to test our code.

Implementing a DAO

This file shows the implementation of the `FilmDao` interface:

Source file: `FilmDaoImpl.java`

```java
package com.packt.dao;

import java.util.List;

import org.hibernate.Session;
import org.hibernate.SessionFactory;
import org.hibernate.Transaction;

import com.packt.modal.Film;

public class FilmDaoImpl implements FilmDao {

  private SessionFactory sessionFactory;

  public FilmDaoImpl(SessionFactory sessionFactory) {
    this.sessionFactory = sessionFactory;
  }

  public void save(Film film) {
    Session session = this.sessionFactory.openSession();
    Transaction tx = session.beginTransaction();
    session.saveOrUpdate(film);
    tx.commit();
    session.close();
  }

  public List<Film> getAll() {
    Session session = this.sessionFactory.openSession();
    List<Film> filmList = session.createQuery("from Film").list();
    session.close();
    return filmList;
  }
}
```

In this file, we only created the two methods that are used to save the file and list all the films.

Creating view – JSP

The `Film.jsp` view is created in the `view` directory, which resides under the `webapp` directory in a traditional web application:

Source file: `film.java`

```
<%@ taglib prefix="s" uri="/struts-tags"%>
<html>
<head>
</head>

<body>
  <h1>Hibernate with Struts 2 integration</h1>

  <h2>Add Film</h2>
  /* Line 10 */ <s:form action="addFilmAction">
    <s:textfield name="name" label="Name" value="" />
    <s:textfield name="releaseYear" label="Release Year" value=""
/>
    <s:submit />
  </s:form>

  <h2>All Films</h2>
  <s:if test="films.size() > 0">
    <table border="1" cellpadding="3">
      <tr>
        <th>Id</th>
        <th>Name</th>
        <th>Release Year</th>
      </tr>
      /* Line 24 */ <s:iterator value="films">
        <tr>
          <td><s:property value="id" /></td>
          <td><s:property value="name" /></td>
          <td><s:property value="releaseYear" /></td>
        </tr>
      </s:iterator>
    </table>
  </s:if>
</body>
</html>
```

This file is returned as an output if the method mapped in `struts.xml` is returned with the desired result tag.

Line `10` creates a Struts form with the `addFilmAction` action, which invokes the `saveFilm` methods of the `com.packt.action.FilmAction` class with the mapping provided in `struts.xml`.

Line `24` accesses the list of the variable films defined in `FilmAction` and renders it as a table using an `iterator`.

How it works...

Let's take a look at how this works for us by running a project.

As this is a web-based application, we will use Apache Tomcat as the server environment to run the project. Tomcat is available under Apache License Version 2 and can be downloaded from `http://tomcat.apache.org/`.

After running the project, we will open the following link in a browser:

`http://localhost:9090/StrutsHibernate/listFilmAction`

Once you open this link, it will display a form asking you to insert the film details. Below this, a list of films will also be displayed. At startup, it shows a blank table as no film records were inserted prior to this, as shown in the following screenshot:

Once you insert any record in the form and click on **Submit**, it will invoke the `saveFilm` method of the `FilmAction` class. This mapping is provided in `struts.xml`. Take a look at the following screenshot:

Once you click on **Submit**, it will submit all the data to the server, and the server will convert all the submitted fields to a Film object and save it to the database. This will also return with all the film records. Take a look at the following screenshot:

See also...

You can read more on Spring integration at:

```
http://docs.spring.io/spring/docs/current/spring-framework-reference/
html/orm.html.
```

Index

autogenerator column
creating 65
default strategy, using 65
sequence generator, using 66
table generator, using 66

B

batch processing
about 195
classes, creating 195-197

C

class
declaring, as hibernate entity 60
column
creating, in table 62
common join table
used, for one-to-one mapping 107
common primary key
used, for one-to-one mapping 112
composite primary key column
creating 64, 65
criteria
creating 46, 47
used, for pagination 50
used, for restricting results 47, 48
**CRUD (Create, Read, Update, Delete)
operation 26**

D

DAO (data access object)
about 199, 200
DAO per class 200
generic DAO or DAO per application 200
database
object, fetching from 36-42
object, removing 42, 43
object, saving 32-36
Data Definition Language (DDL) 2
Data Manipulation Language (DML) 2
default generation strategy
using 65
DI (dependency injection) 199

E

Ehcache distribution
URL 163
Envers 184

F

first-level cache
about 156
classes, getting 157
clear() method 161, 162
evict method 160
properties 156
tables, creating 157-159
foreign key association
used, for one-to-one mapping 98
formula
using, in hibernate 149-152

G

generic SessionFactory provider class
creating 28, 29

H

hbm (hibernate mapping) 10
hibernate
annotation-based hibernate mapping,
providing 12, 13
configuration providing, properties
file used 20, 21
configuration providing, XML file used 18-20
configuring, programmatically 22, 23
features 2
file, manual download 3
JAR (Java Archive) file 3
libraries, getting 3
Maven used 3, 4
POJO (Plain Old Java Object), creating
in Java 4-7
URL 3
XML-based hibernate mapping,
providing 8-12
hibernate persistent class
creating 4-7
HQL (Hibernate Query Language) 129

Thank you for buying
Java Hibernate Cookbook

About Packt Publishing

Packt, pronounced 'packed', published its first book, *Mastering phpMyAdmin for Effective MySQL Management*, in April 2004, and subsequently continued to specialize in publishing highly focused books on specific technologies and solutions.

Our books and publications share the experiences of your fellow IT professionals in adapting and customizing today's systems, applications, and frameworks. Our solution-based books give you the knowledge and power to customize the software and technologies you're using to get the job done. Packt books are more specific and less general than the IT books you have seen in the past. Our unique business model allows us to bring you more focused information, giving you more of what you need to know, and less of what you don't.

Packt is a modern yet unique publishing company that focuses on producing quality, cutting-edge books for communities of developers, administrators, and newbies alike. For more information, please visit our website at www.packtpub.com.

About Packt Open Source

In 2010, Packt launched two new brands, Packt Open Source and Packt Enterprise, in order to continue its focus on specialization. This book is part of the Packt open source brand, home to books published on software built around open source licenses, and offering information to anybody from advanced developers to budding web designers. The Open Source brand also runs Packt's open source Royalty Scheme, by which Packt gives a royalty to each open source project about whose software a book is sold.

Writing for Packt

We welcome all inquiries from people who are interested in authoring. Book proposals should be sent to author@packtpub.com. If your book idea is still at an early stage and you would like to discuss it first before writing a formal book proposal, then please contact us; one of our commissioning editors will get in touch with you.

We're not just looking for published authors; if you have strong technical skills but no writing experience, our experienced editors can help you develop a writing career, or simply get some additional reward for your expertise.

Spring Cookbook

ISBN: 978-1-78398-580-7   Paperback: 234 pages

Over 100 hands-on recipes to build Spring web applications easily and efficiently

1. Build full-featured web applications with Spring MVC.

2. Use Spring 4 Java configuration style to write less code.

3. Learn how to use dependency injection and aspect-oriented programming to write compartmentalized and testable code.

Learning Spring Application Development

ISBN: 978-1-78398-736-8   Paperback: 394 pages

Develop dynamic, feature-rich, and robust Spring-based applications using the Spring Framework

1. Build and deploy Spring-powered, production-grade applications and services with minimal fuss.

2. Discover the key Spring framework-related technology standards such as Spring core, Spring-AOP, Spring data access frameworks, and Spring testing to develop robust Java applications easily and rapidly.

3. A hands-on guide enriched with plenty of diagrams, and Java programs to give you a better understanding of how to design, develop, and test your Spring-based application.

Please check **www.PacktPub.com** for information on our titles

Mastering Spring Application Development

ISBN: 978-1-78398-732-0   Paperback: 288 pages

Gain expertise in developing and caching your applications running on the JVM with Spring

1. Build full-featured web applications, such as Spring MVC applications, efficiently that will get you up and running with Spring web development.

2. Reuse working code snippets handy for integration scenarios such as Twitter, e-mail, FTP, databases, and many others.

3. An advanced guide which includes Java programs to integrate Spring with Thymeleaf.

Mastering Apache Maven 3

ISBN: 978-1-78398-386-5   Paperback: 298 pages

Enhance developer productivity and address exact enterprise build requirements by extending Maven

1. Develop and manage large, complex projects with confidence.

2. Extend the default behavior of Maven with custom plugins, lifecycles, and archetypes.

3. Explore the internals of Maven to arm yourself with knowledge to troubleshoot build issues.

Please check **www.PacktPub.com** for information on our titles

www.ingramcontent.com/pod-product-compliance
Lightning Source LLC
Chambersburg PA
CBHW060541060326
40690CB00017B/3566